DEDICATION

I have been very lucky on my system leader journey to work with so many wonderful colleagues, far too many to mention individually, but I would like to thank every Headteacher from DRET through to Infinity Academies Trust for welcoming me into their school.

I want to give special thanks to G and R for the opportunities that you have given me in 2019/20.

Next, I would like to thank S, J and J for all your support and encouragement in helping me put together this completed book.

Finally thank you to my family, C, J and S, who continue to support me with whatever idea I have.

CONTENTS

ACKNOWLEDGMENTS

Over the last six years I have been fortunate to work in four Multi-Academy Trust.

My first day as a system leader was at Malcolm Arnold Academy in Northampton part of the David Ross Education Trust in January 2015. From there I worked in primary and secondary schools across the DRET network, working with some fantastic Headteachers and System Leaders. Ainthorpe Primary Academy, Edward Heneage Primary Academy and Malcolm Arnold Academy remain close to my heart. Special thanks go to the Northern Primary Heads, my Regional Director Colleagues, the Comms Team, the Sports Team and the many Directors I worked for.

I spent a year with the St Therese of Lisieux CMAT and worked with another a great group of Headteachers and senior leaders where my most enjoyable days began stood at the entrance to St Peter and St Paul's Academy in Lincoln, welcoming the pupils.

My third Trust was The Blessed Peter Snow CMAT with my first days being spent at St John Fisher CVA. I have received a traditional warm Northern welcome in my travels across West Yorkshire.

Last and by no means least is Infinity Academies Trust, a wonderful group of schools filled with great people who I am so proud to be able to support. Thank you to Fiona, Andy, Jo, Sarah and Gavin for all your kindness.

1 FOREWORD

When I began working as a system leader in both secondary and primary schools, I knew that I would be working with fantastic colleagues who were all committed to improving their academies. I also knew that I would be challenged to find solutions to help them to achieve this faster than before. We all recognise that the young people only have one chance and they do not have time to wait.

In all academies, regardless of OFSTED judgement or external outcomes measures, there will always be aspects of the academy that can be improved or fixed. Large-scale change may be required, or it could be the aggregation of marginal gains (the use of many small alterations), which can increase performance.

This book is a collection of the strategies I suggest to the leaders of the schools that I support on a regular basis. I hope you find that these ideas will further fuel your success.

2 INTRODUCTION
NO SILVER BULLETS

We all want our class, our phase, our subject area, our school or our Trust to be the very best it can be. There can be a pressure to find a big idea, implement it properly in the hope that it will transform your setting. The result is that we keep searching for that revolutionary change which will perform the miracle. We look at those schools which are graded as Outstanding, or the schools with the incredible outcomes, or the Trusts that are feted nationally and search for the education elixir, which will have all the answers. These are the mythical silver bullets that we can obsess over.

'the mythical silver bullets…'

Depending on how long you have been in education you will be able to think of some silver bullets, which you may have considered or implemented yourself: from vertical tutor groups to applied ICT qualifications worth multiple GCSE, to learning styles, to a certain phonics scheme. Educationalists who have achieved success with such a change may have claimed that this initiative was the magic panacea.

There is no doubt that such a strategy will have had a positive impact in their school but it does not prove that it will be the magic answer for all schools. It could be argued that the same group of staff would have had same positive impact with a different strategy if they threw themselves into it with the identical passion.

Instead I would argue that there are no secrets to improvement, whether it is of a school or of your own skills. There are no silver bullets and no magic answers. Unfortunately, it is far less glamorous. Instead it is a question of applying effort 'day in, day out' to the improvement that you are making.

'Day in, day out, day in, day out'

There are so many different routes, which you can take on your improvement journey. You may feel that in improving a school you have to change almost everything and give the school a 'fresh start'. The key challenge of leaders in this context is which changes do you begin with?

You could equally believe that the best way forwards is to find one hundred little things and improve them all by one per cent. This is referred to as the 'aggregation of marginal gains.' It could equally be applied to personal development when you are considering which tiny changes you can make to your own actions.

Whether you decide upon complete change, the aggregation of marginal gains or perhaps somewhere in-between, you cannot expect to take an action and not return to it for a while and expect to move forwards, it could move backwards without regular attention. You have to keep working at things 'day in, day out'.

It is with this in mind that during the last five years I have had the privilege of working across over fifty schools, many of them belonging to four Multi Academy Trusts.

I visit schools and aim to coach leaders in how they can improve their school and also pass on little ideas that can help in their work. These are not 'silver bullets.' Neither are they the glamorous big ideas requiring lengthy CPD sessions.

Over the following pages I will share these small actions for you to consider. I hope when you read them you will select some to assist you on your journey to improvement. The more of them that you act upon and return to, the more you can affect school improvement.

Good luck.

[Foot note: On a personal level, 'Day in, day out' is a repeated refrain within the song, 'Digital' sung by the late genius, Ian Curtis as part of the legendary band, Joy Division.]

Where to start?

Whether you have been in your school ten days or ten years it can be difficult to decide where to start in improving the school. There are just so many actions that a leader can take and this book contains a whole variety of them for you to consider.

If you have been in your school a period of time you may believe that you have tried everything to improve your school. We all need to take a fresh view and consider 'is the action embedded in school practice'? If it isn't then we need to return to the issue and hopefully this book could give you the impetus to do so. These small improvements can make a difference in your school to help children.

If you are new to a school it is likely that you have begun the 'due diligence,' which I also complete when I first visit a school. My starting point is to consider performance statistics, as I can often examine this before placing a foot over the threshold by looking at the historic available data. We can look at attainment and progress outcomes, attendance and exclusion figures, pupil numbers, finance in some cases, OFSTED reports and there is lots of further information on the school website.

This analysis of a range of school performance indicators allows us to begin to consider areas where improvements could be made. When we actually walk into the school we will constantly be evaluating the provision that we see before us. This could be informal observation from being in the building and viewing what we see around us. It could be a more formal process through completing individual self-evaluation tools (learning walks, lesson observations, pupil voice, work scrutiny, observing pupils during less formal moments in the school day). You may take this a step further and triangulate, through deep dives in certain subject areas, or by completing a review.

You will have the most recent tracking data in whatever form it is presented. Whilst the new OFSTED framework suggests that inspectors will no longer ask for in-year outcomes, most leaders will wish to have their method of determining whether pupils are on-track for their targets. If I visit a school as a system leader, I often request this data and will continue to do so. In addition, there will be current information on attendance, behaviour logs and exclusions, which you can examine.

From all this evidence we will be taking a view on the attainment and progress outcomes, which the children have achieved historically and possibly in-year. We can look at the quality of teaching and learning so that outcomes improve quickly and gaps are closed rapidly. These elements are now encompassed in OFSTED's 'Quality of Education.' We will also be assessing the behaviour of students and how this supports learning. Finally, we will wish that the attendance is high, as if the young people are not in the building then they cannot learn. These latter two now fall under the OFSTED's banner of 'Behaviour and Attitudes.' This guide though is not about improving your OFSTED judgement: this is about taking actions to make improvements for your children.

You may have a firm view as to where you need to start, be it quality first teaching, behaviour or attendance. You may also wish to apply some short-term sticking plasters to boost pupil outcomes to try and gain some quick improvement. This is not a long-term sustainable strategy but there are occasions in a school's improvement journey when it is necessary.

The strategies in this book are grouped against these four areas so that when you conduct your self-evaluation and find gaps in performance you can quickly refer to the appropriate section. You can consider which are already being used and can be tweaked or which you can implement anew.

3 DEVELOPING QUALITY FIRST TEACHING

Most school leaders will rightly say that the most important part of school improvement is raising the quality of teaching and learning in the school. There are many different vehicles to do this, some of which are available to purchase. These include processes like 'Direct Instruction' included in 'Teach like a Champion' by Doug Lemov to TEEP, a strategy used by many schools to planning tools such as 'the 5minute lesson plan' from Teacher Toolkit. These provide methods which you can hang your approach on for teaching and learning at your school.

This chapter does not suggest such a whole scale strategy for teaching and learning but instead is based on lots of little actions that you can utilise to make marginal improvements. If you are already a TEEP school or a Direct Instruction school, you can still use these actions to make further improvements.

The following table allows you to track which actions you have implemented over the course of the academic year. The majority of actions are suitable for primary and secondary school with only a small number focussed on one phase. Again, you must return to them at least termly to ensure 'stickability.'

You can then ask yourself two questions:

- What has been the impact?

- What do we need to do differently to maintain / increase the impact?

Figure 3.1: Summary of actions to develop quality first teaching

	Action	Primary	Secondary	T1	T2	T3
1	Check the planned curriculum is being followed	*	*			
2	Ensure the curriculum is being delivered according to the year group expectations	*	*			
3	Ensure that teachers are adapting learning, meeting the needs of all learners	*	*			
4	Consistent timetable on the outside of classroom doors	*	*			
5	Consistent approach to learning walls	*				
6	Ensure teachers have plans in place to address the gaps	*	*			
7	'Book is king!'	*	*			
8	Overcoming learning barriers	*	*			

9	Is teaching targeting pupils in vulnerable groups?	*	*			
10	Addressing gaps in phonics	*				
11	Weekly focus in EYFS	*				
12	Curriculum structure in EYFS	*				
13	Less is more!	*				
14	Opportunities for outdoor mark-making	*				
15	Deploy subject leads to model good and outstanding teaching	*	*			
16	Ensure there is a system of coaching to improve teaching	*	*			
17	Using standardised assessment	*	*			
18	How are assessments quality assured?	*	*			
19	Judging quality of teaching and learning	*	*			
20	Work scrutiny as a vehicle for improvement	*	*			
21	Calendar learning walks and formal observations	*	*			

22	Use lesson observations to support improvement	*	*			
23	Clear systems for pupil progress or raising achievement group meetings.	*	*			
24	Ensure pupil progress meetings focus on the skills that individual children need	*	*			
25	Triangulating evidence.	*	*			
26	Group staff according to grade and determine when support is needed	*	*			
27	Prioritise senior leaders to model effective teaching	*	*			
28	Moving from monitoring to development	*	*			

DEVELOPING QUALITY FIRST TEACHING

THE ACTIONS

Action 1:

Check the planned curriculum is being followed

It may appear obvious to all leaders that the planned curriculum is being followed and hence this action belongs under the category of assume nothing and check everything. Every year teachers will have conversations with leaders after examinations, bemoaning the fact that certain questions have arisen in exams and they haven't covered that material. Yet this must be the tip of the iceberg as these are the groups who are having external examinations, there will be many other years in the school who are not being tested in this way, hence what check is there that the curriculum is being followed. If we extrapolate from the external examination groups there must be many other year groups who have missed material.

Action 49 in the following section asked you to consider whether long term planning covered the entire curriculum. The best plans in the world will not be effective if they are not being delivered.

In some Multi Academy Trusts, curriculum specialists using a considerable investment will have designed a standardised curriculum. Yet in individual schools and classrooms you can often find that teachers are not delivering the curriculum which has been designed, and hence all that time and investment is being wasted.

You can also find that teachers will are not affording the appropriate timing to the curriculum. Typically, the material at the start of the year has more time has been spent on it and then the end of the year can be rushed. If the same topic area is placed at the end of the year for different year groups, they can have a large gap in their knowledge for this particular strand of the curriculum.

What can you do?

Just as you used a line management meeting at the beginning of year to check that the curriculum gave full coverage of either the examination syllabus or the national curriculum, during subsequent line management meetings discuss with middle leaders and teachers the progress they are making in covering the curriculum.

Are time scales set in the plans being kept to? Does it look realistic that the material will be covered at appropriate points? Can you triangulate between the progress that different teachers are making to check that the curriculum is not being rushed?

'Planned curriculum prevents gaps in delivery'

Action 2

Ensure the curriculum is being delivered according to the year group / ability expectations

This action is very similar to the previous one and could have been covered through the planning that has been completed. In primary settings it is really important that the children are being taught the appropriate year group expectations.

With the implementation of mastery curriculum in Math's it is now rare for teachers to deliver the curriculum in the year above, as there is so much material available for extending the reasoning skills of children.

Leaders must though ensure that teachers are not reducing the expectations by consistently delivering material from the year groups below. If children have received poor teaching previously, teachers may feel they have gaps to fill but they must be accelerating progress, as otherwise children will always remain behind.

In secondary settings, it is likely that curriculum areas will have designed differentiated schemes of work. If there are ability sets, then it is likely that those children in higher sets will receive a different diet of content than those in lower sets.

It is important to check that children are being challenged in appropriate ways and that the wrong ceiling is not being placed on the children's learning. The same can be true if the material is too challenging and children are being rushed through the learning and they are not retaining the knowledge. Such is the rush to reach the end of the syllabus.

What can you do?

When you are reviewing planning and the progress being made during the year, discuss which year group expectations are being followed and how the children are coping with this.

In secondary schools, have similar conversations about the diet, which different children are receiving, and any limits this could place on their future outcomes.

'All children should receive an aspirational curriculum'

Action 3:

Ensure that teachers are adapting learning, meeting the needs of all learners

We all understand that in all classrooms, learners are at different stages of their development whether that is a mixed age primary class or a secondary school subject with sets.

In addition, there will be children with personalised targets, these could be informal in different support plans, through to SEND Individual Education Plans (IEPs) through to the very formal Education Health Care Plan (EHCP).

Teachers must therefore ensure that learning is adapted to meet the needs of all learners of all classrooms rather than being a one size fits all model and all that changes is the outcomes of the learning for different pupils.

Leaders must therefore monitor what is happening in the classrooms to ensure that adaptations are being made so that all learners can make good progress.

One of the keys to meeting the needs of all learners is how teachers differentiate for the pupils in the class. Five commonly understood forms of differentiation are by:
- Task
- Outcome
- Questioning
- Resource
- Support

What can you do?

Every year ensure that there is CPD on how teachers can meet the need of all learners. Never assume that this is something that all staff can do. In addition, the annual coverage of this topic means that it stays at the forefront of all teachers' minds.

Ensure that medium term planning has suggestions for the routes different learners will take through the topics and what their outcomes will be.

When learning walks occur ensure that meeting all needs of all learners is a continual focus. Praise staff when you see good practice and encourage them to share these techniques with their colleagues around them.
If a colleague appears to be struggling with this area, signpost colleagues who manage this well and give them opportunities to observe this good practice.

'Meeting the needs of learners is key to effective provision'

Action 4:

Consistent timetables on the outside of classroom doors

When some Headteachers are asked what is happening at a certain point in time in their school, they will return to their office and point out timetables for each class on a noticeboard or they may reach for a folder on their shelf and show a set of brightly coloured timetables.

If they are then asked how much time is given to a certain subject, they may have another document where they have completed an audit of each subject area or they may have to complete the calculation.

If there is a learning walk of a school, it is often found that at some point the Headteacher will be surprised by the subject or activity that is being completed in a certain classroom. In addition, if the observer wishes to look at reading across the school, they will have spread the learning walk over a range of times in a day to see all the classes.

What can you do?

One solution is to create a consistent whole school timetable particularly for the core subjects in the morning. This formalises that all classes have their Maths lesson at the same time, then their writing lesson at the same time and also their reading / phonics lesson at the same time.

Some schools also include spelling and timetables activities as discrete items on the timetable too. This makes it very straightforward to ensure that teachers are not favouring one subject over another and that pupils are receiving an equitable amount of time for all their learning.

There will be some complications with activities such as swimming that may take place in the morning for one class one day a week and the timetable will have to be adjusted in the light of this.

Leaders do not even have to walk into the classroom as they may able to look through the window and observe where children have reached in their day's learning.

Monitoring is equally simple in that you can look at a subject such as Maths by using the same hour to walk through classrooms. Pitch and challenge across the school is also much easier to assess.

A school can take this a stage further by asking teachers at the beginning of each week to include their learning intention for each lesson on the timetable. They can write an amendment to this if it changes based on the outcome of the previous lesson. Leaders can evaluate long term planning by reading these objectives rather than having to hunt through planning templates.

'Common timetables enable quick and easy monitoring of quality'

Action 5:

Consistent approach to learning walls

It is always fascinating to look at the different approaches primary teachers take to displays in their classrooms. It often feels that there is a triangle of intentions for such displays.

Displays can be very decorative. In this case they can be exciting and stimulating to the children. One example might be the display about the class text which is being covered. The second aim could be to display children's work so that the children and other visitors to the classroom can see the best efforts of the children. The third aim is as a learning wall, which should change regularly and support the learning during that week.

What can you do?

In any classroom you will wish to see a balance between the three different factors of displays. You will want to see some really high-quality displays which may stay in place for a half term and inspire the children. You will also want to see work by the children celebrated.

In Reading, Writing and Mathematics though you may wish the noticeboards to be working, learning walls. This may mean that they are more functional in style and may not be as artistic in nature because they are changing every day to support the learning intentions in that particular lesson.

Some schools will approach this in Maths by using flip chart papers. In each Maths lesson the skill for the lesson is modelled on flip chart paper. On the Maths learning wall will be flip chart papers from the two previous lessons. At the start of the lesson the teacher can refer to the work from previous lessons, recap what has been learnt and then use this as a springboard into the new lesson as they begin to model on a new flip chart paper. Then at the end of the lesson the oldest flip chart paper is removed and the one from that day replaces it.

Teachers can use a similar approach in guided reading. In writing the learning wall may develop over a fortnight as a piece of writing displayed on the wall is unpacked and a new piece of writing is built up and modelled over the fortnight before the pupils then try and produce their own.

These systems can be extremely helpful in monitoring as leaders can quickly look at the learning walls to see what has been covered in previous lessons, how it fits with medium term planning and also if it matches the timetable on the classroom door.

'A system of learning walls can support both teacher and leaders'

Action 6:

Ensure teachers have plans in place to address the gaps

One of the key questions following pupil progress meeting is ensuring that teachers have plans in place to address the gaps and that there is also a system in place which monitors whether those gaps have been filled.

Leaders do not wish to wait a term or half a term and find in the next pupil progress meeting that pupils have the identical omissions in their learning that they had last time.

The only way to avoid this is to ensure that teachers have plans and a monitoring strategy to check whether they have been successful.

What can you do?

At the end of the pupil progress meeting ensure that teachers have a simple proforma, with an identified learning objective for each child, which has been taught, but they have not currently met.

If a number of pupils have the same issue, then work with the teacher to ensure that there is a point in the day when they will address this issue with the group of pupils. The other pupils may be working on an independent activity whilst this is being completed. In a primary environment, there is likely to be teamwork between the teacher and teaching assistant to facilitate this gap filling.

If only one child has a specific gap, then the teacher needs to plan at what point during the day, they will find the opportunity to work on this with the child. Again, in primary schools there is likely to be joint approach with the TA.

You could also consider if there are other adults who can help fill these gaps. Could senior leaders work with small groups or individual pupils on behalf of the class teacher? This should be a timetabled on a regular basis.

There needs to be a re-assessment point with the children to see if they have retained this knowledge. This could be a whole class activity where the teacher makes an assessment comprising of all the gaps they are filling or it could be individual / small group assessment.

'Use leaders to support the class teacher with interventions'

Action 7:

'Book is king'

One of the most effective methods I have seen for raising the profile of high-quality learning is the idea that 'book is king'. This means that the best outcome of children's learning over the course of the year is what is in their books. Hence in turn if you wish to see the progress that the children are making look through the books and see the improvement that the children are making and the new ideas that they are learning and applying.

Primary schools have been particularly effective at using this technique and the pupils' books show a great deal of care from the teacher and the child. Both are extremely proud of what is in them. The care begins with the front covers with house style labels on them. Some schools will use clear plastic covers akin to those used in libraries. Other schools have invested in hard-back books, which seem more similar to Artist's sketchbooks than exercise books.

When you open the books, you see the same level of care. Many schools use the idea of cold writes and hot writes. The cold write is a task that pupils undertake before they have begun the topic and the hot write at the end of the topic, which then shows all the progress that the children have made. Some schools will only assess these two tasks; everything in between will be self-marking, peer marking and live marking.

The same system has been used in secondary schools especially if outcomes have been very low and this gives the school an opportunity to show the progress the children are making. At the same time, it can build children's confidence as they can have a physical demonstration of the new material they have learnt.

What can you do?

The first element of 'book is king' is to explain the theory of the practice and highlight that there are no excuses; everybody has to show care in the books. When this is not shown, it needs to be addressed.

There needs to simple expectations of how books will be presented which is agreed and used across the school. You can implement your own system of 'cold' and 'hot' tasks, which capture the progress that children make in their learning.

Talk to children with their books about their learning. Ask them to show you elements that they are proud of, things that they have learnt and also where they have overcome difficulties.

'Pupil books present the story of school effectiveness'

Action 8:

Overcoming learning barriers

In a previous point, it was asked if teaching is targeting vulnerable pupils and the key to this is that their learning barriers are being overcome.

In your school are you clear how the different elements of the curriculum, help pupil overcome these barriers? For example, do teachers understand how they should assess EAL pupils to find out what elements of their learning needs addressing first? Are teachers aware of the different resources that they should use with EAL pupils according to what the assessment tells them? If the pupils are not making progress, does the teacher know what provision should then be provided? Equally if the child is making accelerated progress what should they do next?

In a primary school this type of mapping needs to be completed for different areas of the curriculum and in a secondary school, subject areas will need to have planned approaches.

In terms of training are staff regularly trained on techniques, which they need to implement to overcome certain barriers.? New teachers will arrive in your school and those that remain they may forget certain techniques so such training needs to be completed regularly.

What can you do?

The key barriers to learning in your school need to be identified. Each school will have different issues with varying levels of need.

Ensure there are planned approaches for dealing with different learning barriers. The different curriculum resources need to be detailed and amended over time so that teachers know where to find appropriate materials and also so that there is a school wide approach to dealing with barriers rather than each individual teacher finding their own way.

Have a planned delivery of training so that the teacher's knowledge is regularly refreshed and that the school keep up to date with the most recent best practice.

'Overcoming barriers is not easy and a planned approach will be most effective.'

Action 9:

Is teaching targeting pupils in vulnerable groups?

Two key elements to your school's improvement is to ensure that the children in vulnerable groups are firstly not falling further behind and secondly that they are making up for any lost ground that they have from previous Key Stages.

You will have your own definition of vulnerable groups of pupils. It could be those that we are used to such as pupil premium, SEN, EAL or LAC children.

It could be a group of children that is specific to your school, such as pupils in a certain prior attainment group, or a group of children that you identified from the previous year of falling behind the expected attainment.

To check that teaching is targeting these pupils you need to have a slightly more sophisticated approach to evaluating what is happening in classrooms.

What can you do?

Firstly, for each class you need to have a list of those pupils that you consider vulnerable and for what reason so that you can keep track of their progress.

When you are completing lesson drop ins, check on some of those vulnerable pupils. For example, do they require differentiated materials to support them? Can they access what is available for the rest of the class and if so are the expectations high enough?

Are such pupils always with Teaching Assistants or are they also receiving input from the classroom teacher? The Teaching Assistant may be highly skilled but the teacher should also be providing input.

When you look in books, is the standard of work appropriate and are they making good progress? Ensure that on each book look a sample of the vulnerable pupils is being considered.

During pupil progress meetings are the needs of vulnerable pupils being considered and is there clarity on the gaps they have and what actions are required to fill them?

'Don't assume that the needs of vulnerable pupils are being met'

Action 10:

Addressing gaps in phonics

Whilst pupil progress meetings are a regular part of practice in Key Stage 2 they are less regularly used in supporting the learning for phonics checks. Yet in many ways, pupil progress meetings are well suited for use in year 1 and also when looking at pupils in year 2 who are retaking the phonics test.

A number of phonics schemes operate with children being placed in different small groups according to their progress. Such groups are not determined by the age of the pupil but instead at what stage their phonics learning is. To try and create groups as small as possible, it is not unusual for TAs from other classes to be involved in this short lesson often at the beginning of the day.

Regular phonics assessments will then identify the specific learning objectives, which pupils are working towards.

What can you do?

Firstly, if you are taking a small group approach, do not assume that pupils should continually remain in the same group. Pupils will develop at different rates and there will be occasions when pupils can be moved up a group or may need moving down a group if their learning is stalling.

Ensure that one colleague is taking responsibility for phonics across the school and they will then conduct short pupil progress meetings with the colleagues who are working with the children. This should encompass TAs as well as classroom teachers.

Implement a system of phonics mocks that is in-line with those discussed in action 45 using a trajectory model of marks. The assessments should be completed in the same style that the final assessment would take place as discussed in action 52.

Ensure the learning objectives which are proving a barrier to the child's learning are recorded.

Provide a system where adults will address these barriers at points within the school day. It may be as simple as the class TA having a list of the barriers and over the course of a week ensures that they give some 1:1 teaching on this barrier during the school day.

'Addressing phonics barriers should be achieved through teamwork'

Action 11:

Weekly foci in EYFS

In all EYFS setting it can be a challenge to ensure that during 'free play' / 'child-initiated learning' all children are making progress towards a 'good level of development.'

For those settings firmly wedded to providing a range of opportunities across different areas, how do you ensure that the same children do not always go to construction activities and do not choose mark making? What about the children who are eager to use the role play area but are less prepared to make use of shape and space activities?

When you visit a large EYFS setting which does not have discrete areas for classes of children, this can be even more challenging to assess as there will be many different adults spread over the classroom space, both indoor and outside.

What can you do?

Some schools have taken the idea of pupil progress meetings and developed the concept into a more fluid mechanism, which is more in keeping with an EYFS setting.

Each week the adults in the setting will identify a number of target children with the aim that over a period of six weeks all children will have been chosen. In an ideal world it is best if this is over a shorter time such as a four-week period but it depends on the ratio of adults to children.

Then for each target child, the adults will discuss what the barriers to learning are, what activities they prefer and which activities they rarely choose. From this the practitioners will highlight areas and activities, which they wish to encourage the child to participate in.

During the week the practitioners will look for opportunities to encourage the target children to develop their learning. They will make records of the progress that is being made by the target children, in addition to their normal routine record keeping.

Towards the end of the week, the records of the target children will be collated. In some settings they will try and arrange short meetings with the parents of the target children to explain the progress their child has made that week and the different activities they have engaged with. There may also be a short-written communication, which is given to parents who they are not able to meet with.

'Steer the target children for that week towards different activities to develop their learning'

Action 12:

Curriculum structure in EYFS

When you look at the GLD assessments or the current tracking towards GLD, you may notice that some children seem to be making better progress towards certain learning goals than others.

As a leader when you are monitoring, you may consider that certain elements of provision are far more developed than others. For example, there may be a very rich set of opportunities for mark making both inside and outside, but those for number are more limited.

As a teacher you may feel that you are stronger in working on some aspects of learning than others and hence those learning activities are more vibrant.

Some settings may have imbalance in terms of gender or another pupil grouping which means that certain activities are accessed more frequently than others. It is a controversial topic but some practitioners may feel that due to the learning opportunities children have accessed in the setting prior to school they are not always able to make best use of a wide range of opportunities.

In these circumstances, practitioners have developed more structure to their setting to ensure that is made more manageable for all children to access all activities.

What can you do?

Many EYFS settings will divide their morning into sessions perhaps with a snack in between. They will then allocate one of the sessions towards numeracy and one towards literacy.

For the numeracy session there will be a range of activities available to promote an element of numeracy. There can be games, mark making, construction and role play activities. These are the activities that will be available for the week and practitioners will aim to guide the children around the activities over the week so that all children have the opportunity to experience each of them.

In the second session of the morning, the numeracy activities will be put away and a similar process will take place with the literacy activities for the week. A range of literacy activities will be available and again the children will be encouraged to participate in them over the week.

You may also find that monitoring the progress children are making becomes more straight forwards too.

'Consider what structure you provide in EYFS and whether this would support the learning in your context'

Action 13:

Less is more!

How many times have you been in an Early Years Setting, inside or outside and been astonished by the vast range of material available? For children it can be like being in the biggest sweet shop in the world and they just do not know where to start with their free play. The result is that children can flit aimlessly from one resource to another, getting it out and then moving onto the next resource, rather than gaining the full learning benefit.

Many practitioners will also say that if it can be seen, children should be able to use it, so those items that are in clear boxes on shelves are also taken out adding to the over stimulation.

The same can be true in the outdoor area. Though outside what you can see is that children move to the same activity, which they do day after day. This is often seen with items such as bicycles that children love riding and every day they rush to use them.

What can you do?

At the start of the year, have a limited range of resources out available for children. In addition, for each resource, do not have all of it out. During the year increase the quantity and variation of individual resources as children become more adept at playing with them. A good example is with indoor construction resources, you will begin with the larger bricks and as the year progresses you will bring out smaller resources, which require more fine motor skills.

Ensure that resources are stored in cupboards with doors so that you can choose when is the appropriate point in the year. This may mean that earlier on in the year there will be reduced resources at child level on shelves.

In the outside area, make sure there is a shed where larger materials can be stored and again you can choose when to bring them out.

In addition, rotate some of the larger resources outside especially items like bicycles or larger cars. Children will use a greater range of materials outside and hence develop wider skills.

'Rotate resources during the year and store them out of sight'

Action 14:

Opportunities for out-door mark-making

In so many schools the performance of boys is an issue and needs to be addressed as soon as they begin school. Drilling down into boys' performance, it can often be the writing where there are significant gaps.

When children enter primary school there can already be gaps between boys and girls and this can be characterised in fine motor skills. The ability to hold pens and pencils and have co-ordination can be lacking.

There are many schools that have had these gaps and have made considerable progress with boys' writing through having a rich range of resources for children to complete mark making outside. Yet still there are schools where this is an underdeveloped area.

Even when schools have beautiful outside resources with purposeful built trim tails, outdoor kitchens and even marked out roads, there may be no clear opportunities for children to begin their writing with giant letters.

What can you do?

Resources for mark making do not have to be expensive but they do have to be planned so that children who are reluctant to mark make inside, are given lots of encouragement to work at scale outside.

Ensure you have easels outside with flip chart paper on them with the appropriate resources to write on them, be that chunky colouring pencils and crayons, paint brushes or even washable marker pens.

Have large paintbrushes or wallpaper paste brushes with water so that children can write and draw with water on the floor.

Are the chalkboards mounted at the low level on exterior walls so that children can use chalk on them to make patterns?

Can there be implements, which release a powder such as flour and sand, which children can draw with?

As with Action 13, 'less is more in EYFS' you will not have every resource out every day and children will need to be guided to use them. Ensure that every day different opportunities are provided.

'Outdoor mark making is the starting point of children's writing'

Action 15:

Deploy subject leads to model good and outstanding teaching

In education we often talk about a 'WAGOLL'. If you have not heard that acronym, it means 'What a good one looks like'. If we do not know what the proverbial 'good one' looks like, how do we really know whether what we are producing is good?

If you are a senior leader, you are probably very aware of what good or effective teaching looks like in practice. You may have received Inset on what to look for and you will regularly visit other classrooms to see teaching in practice. Even if you lack confidence in definitively stating what is effective practice, you will be able to order teaching in terms of effectiveness. The same may not be true for all your teachers.

If you think about the colleagues teaching in your school, those teachers without responsibility will be spending 90% of the time teaching lessons with the other 10% being used towards their planning and preparation for the week. How often do they get to observe other teachers? How often do they actually get to see what a good lesson looks like?

In many primary schools whilst classroom teachers deliver all subjects there will be a subject lead who has a particular strength and interest in that subject. In secondary school within each subject area there will be a subject lead. As a leader you need to try to ensure that these leads have an impact on teaching and learning beyond their classroom.

What can you do?

You need to find ways of giving opportunities for a range of teachers to observe subject leads either teaching their own class or modelling practice in the classroom of another teacher.

Can you cover either your teacher or the subject lead so that the teacher can observe the subject lead? If you leave it purely to when teachers have PPA it may not be convenient to see the particular subject being delivered.

Paired observation can be really helpful as teachers may need support on what to look or conversation around what it would look like in their classroom.

In a secondary school could you have an open classroom week with a timetable of when colleagues can observe subject leads teach? Each teacher then has to sign up to observe a subject lead. If you include this in your 1265 audit you can use directed time for this purpose so colleagues are not using their PPA time, which they could object to.

'Find opportunities for teachers to observe high quality delivery'

Action 16:

Ensure there is a system of coaching to improve teaching

Many educationalists believe that the best method of improving teaching is either one to one coaching or coaching triads. Colleagues work with each other to observe practice and then advise on actions to make improvement.

There are lots of different systems of coaching. Some schools will train certain teachers or leaders to be coaches. They will then be given a coaching workload of colleagues that they are working with to improve their practice.

A very different model is to train all teachers as coaches and develop a model of peer coaching which could be one to one or in triads. Some schools will use a combination of the two models so that those colleagues who require support work with specialist coaches and those teachers who are effective will work in peer triads.

Just as there are different organisational systems for coaching there are also different styles of coaching, which can be used. Some colleagues will favour the style of coaching, which Paul Bambrick-Santoyo explains in 'Leverage Leadership'. This is very directive with the coach tells the teachers what they need to improve upon and together they model the practice.

Other colleagues will favour coaching that uses models like 'Grow' or 'TGROW' where the coach works alongside the teacher and helps them to find solutions and works with them to overcome barriers.

What do you need to do?

As a leader you need to research different organisational systems of coaching and decide which will work best in your setting. This could be influenced by the number of teachers you have and what the immediate needs of the teachers are.

You also need to consider what style of coaching you think fits best with the culture of your school and where it is on its development cycle.

Finally, you need to ensure that training is delivered for coaches so that they can coach effectively. Do not assume that a great teacher will make a great coach; this is not always the case.

There are lots of books and blogs that cover coaching in great detail, which will help you on the journey.

'Coaching is one of the most effective ways of improving teaching'

Action 17:

Using standardised assessments

Many schools are very nervous about purely using teacher assessments to understand the progress that children in the school are currently making. There will be others who say that as OFSTED is no longer asking for current tracking data in the school then why should school leaders?

Leaders will explain that if they and teachers do not know where children have reached from one year to the next, how can teachers then build on the learning, not only during the year but also when they gain a new class at the start at the academic year?

The idea of using previous SATs paper and GCSE papers will be discussed in chapter 4 along with gaining an understanding of the trajectory that a child is on. (Action 45). In the past some schools have used GCSE papers in Key Stage 3 or KS2 SATs papers in the years 3, 4 and 5 as a method of assessing the progress of these children. Yet this is not what those papers were designed to do and many data experts will suggest this method is flawed.

What can you do?

Introduce a series of standardised assessments during the year, whether this is one at the end of the school year or one at the end of each full term. The latter is used in many primary schools. The following suggests four models which can be implemented.

The school could design their assessments using the programmes of study. This method works if you wish to find out what the children have learnt over the year and what gaps they have but is not suitable for determining what the pupils are on track to achieve at the end of KS2 or KS4.

In primary settings there are a number of commercially produced standardised assessments ranging from PIRA / PUMA tests to NFER assessments. They all have their own advantages and disadvantages and importantly in the current climate, one is their cost. Some are online which can reduce marking load.

In secondary settings many of the examination boards produce assessments for different years in a range of subjects, which are also standardised and give grade boundaries.

The PiXL group also has their own assessments with a large data set, which can be used at both primary and secondary.

'Standardised tests are an important tool in determining the pupils' trajectory'

Action 18:

How are assessments quality assured?

There are some schools that collect assessment or tracking data six times a year across the whole range of subjects, be it primary or secondary school. This information is then used in pupil progress meetings to check the progress of pupils against the school targets.

This information may take many different forms. Teachers may input current working grades, a prediction grade, the grade a child is on track to achieve or even the 'flight path' a child is on.

The question that leaders then need to ask it what are the assessment grades based on? How is this quality assured? In action 45 consideration will be given to the accuracy of historical grades and a suggestion was given of how mock information for year 6 and year 11 can be used with a system to quality assure predictions. Here we are asking about other year groups.

If this information is not quality assured then teachers in year 6 and year 11 can feel that they do not have accurate information to begin upon which they can build learning.

What can you do?

In primary schools these teacher assessments are often based on what the children have achieved in lessons. For those schools with commercial tracking systems, after each objective has been covered, the teacher will assess whether the pupil has met that objective.

From this information, the teacher will judge whether the pupil is at the expected standard, above or below it. There may be more gradations than this.

The quality assurance process for the teacher assessment can be achieved by looking at a sample of books, two at the standard, two above and two below and consideration can be given to whether the books show objectives being met, additional challenges being met or objectives not being met.

In secondary, there can be the temptation to give a test each half term which can increase workload, especially in schools who are doing this every half term for every child. A school could use the same process as in primaries of quality assuring the books, which links with the concept of 'Book is King', action 7.

Equally there may be an assessment, which is completed in class or at home. It is useful for teachers and middle leaders to produce a template, which explains for each assessment point what the assessment is based on and how it is being quality assured.

'Tracking data must be quality assured to best inform future teaching'

Action 19:

Judging the quality of teaching and learning

It is important to understand how strengths and weaknesses in teaching and learning are being assessed or determined. Assessing the quality of teaching and learning will not bring about improvement on its own; instead it is the actions that leaders take following this. If no assessment is being made then leaders will not know where, or even if, they have to take action.

The new OFSTED handbook has the opportunity to confuse this issue further. There was considerable debate amongst school leaders as to whether individual teachers should be graded at all. All leaders had their own view upon this but they could still consider which teachers were not delivering 'Good' teaching.

The new handbook does not have its own separate judgement on teaching and learning but instead this will be considered under the implementation strand of the 'quality of education' and the impact strand of the quality of education'.

For many schools this means that rather than grading teaching, they can instead focus on looking at individual teachers and considering what strengths do they have in their teaching and also what areas of improvement they may have.

Some schools have begun to use career stage expectations and have divided up the teacher standards into a range of steps, which teachers will be on according to how far they have reached in their career.

The next stage is to consider if there are strengths, are the ways in which they can support improvement across the school. If there are areas of improvement, is that just an issue for that individual teacher and hence can be worked on individually? Or is it an area than a number of colleagues are struggling with and in which case, can this be something that can be looked upon as a wider CPD initiative?

What can you do?

Work with your teachers to determine how you will judge teaching. Whatever system you decide to use, try to keep it as simple as possible so that it is easily explained and teachers are not confused by the process. Share your system with colleagues in the school and then consider what the process over the course of the year will look like.

'Who are your best teachers and who need your support?'

Action 20:

Work scrutiny as a vehicle for improvement

In many schools, work scrutiny does not have a positive connotation. Instead it has been used as method to 'beat staff' over whether every piece of pupil work has been marked. Many school staff would dread seeing work scrutiny on the school calendar and the days leading up to it would become a nightmarish process of constant marking.

It is highly debateable whether such leadership practice is a supporting school improvement or instead just contributing to the demotivation and burn out of staff.

This does not mean you should not do work scrutiny but instead the challenge is to ensure that it becomes a vehicle for school improvement.

Work scrutiny has a number of aims. The first is to check the quality of pupil's work and see if it is as expected by the school. The second is to ensure compliance with a school policy, whether that is a marking policy or a feedback policy. The third is using it as a method of sharing good practice.

What can you do?

Ensure that work scrutiny is calendared regularly to encourage teachers to continually reflect on how they are addressing your school's feedback policy. If it is a once a term thing, this can create over load.

Be very clear as to what you are looking for from the work scrutiny. This should be checking that 'book is king' and that the progress the pupil is making is seen in the book, rather than checking every single piece of product from a child is 'marked'.

Do not have work scrutiny as a secret activity but always involve a range of colleagues including middle and senior leaders. Some schools will make work scrutiny a whole staff event; in small schools, teachers will gather and share books and in large schools this may be based on groups of colleagues. This has been described as a 'bring and brag' approach with teachers then setting next steps for each other too. For each of these methods you should ensure that colleagues look at different set of books.

Use small sample sizes so it is a speedy process and just ensure that each time a different sample is used from each teacher.

Look for good practice that can be shared particularly around reducing workload and try to ensure that each work scrutiny finds at least one practical strategy, which can be shared across the school.

'Use work scrutiny to share good practice'

Action 21:

Calendar learning walks and formal lesson observations

Most leaders would agree that for teaching to remain at a high standard it needs to be observed and then feedback given to colleagues on how it can be improved and at the same time strengths commented on.

This is best done through both formal lesson observations and shorter learning walks. The formal lesson observation allows more detail to be teased out and provides both colleagues greater opportunity to discuss what they have seen and share ideas for the future. However, learning walks tend to be more about the typicality of what is occurring in the classroom.

Every year I work with schools that have been through some type of review process both internal and external and are surprised at the outcomes of the process. They have presumed certain elements are occurring in the classroom and then realise that this was not happening for a whole host of reasons.

It is often at this point a conversation will be held with leaders about learning walks and lesson observations and it is found that they are either not occurring in a planned or focussed manner. They may be happening regularly but the colleague has gained a flavour of the relationships between teacher and child but not the actual learning that has occurred.

What can you do?

Publish a programme of learning walks and formal lesson observations for the whole calendar year and ensure it is someone's role to make sure these happen rather than slipping by the wayside, as life gets busy, as it always will.

Ensure there are simple proformas that the observer completes and they share the outcomes with teachers.

You may also decide to include your own system of 'deep dives' into this process but remember 'deep dives' will be a time-consuming process and if you try to do too many over the year, you could find that it becomes difficult to ensure that learning walks and lesson observations continue on a regular basis.

'Quality assurance needs to triangulated, planned and calendared'

Action 22:

Use lesson observation to support improvement

In action 21, it was suggested that leaders ensure that there is a published calendar of observations both formal and learning walks and that a colleague took responsibility for ensuring they occur.

Lesson observation can prove to be one of the most powerful methods of improved teaching quality. This is recognised for trainee teachers at the start of their career but as soon as teachers qualify and begin employment the opportunities for observation let alone focussed observation is greatly limited. Instead observation becomes the preserve of leaders making judgements and hopefully working to improve the practice of the teacher being observed.

If leaders instead begin to consider how can observation be used to improve the practice of other teachers in the school, schools can utilise some of the most powerful and cost effective CPD in the school.

What can you do?

Ensure that all lessons are observed by two colleagues; a leader and a less experienced, or less skilled practitioner.

The observer then has two roles in the observation. The first is to look at the teacher they are observing to determine strengths and areas for improvement of this teacher that can be looked at following the observation. The second is to work with their joint observer to discuss what they are watching and how this can be applied to improving the practice of the second observer.

If strengths and areas of improvements of teachers are already identified, then you can select the second observer so their areas for improvement match with the strengths of the teacher is being observed.

This type of observation can also be used within a support plan if a teacher has a particular area which they need to develop. They can observe a colleague who is well versed in this element of teaching and hopefully gain ideas, which they can take away and use in their classroom.

'Observation is one of the most powerful tools for improving Teaching'

Action 23:

'Clear systems for
Pupil Progress / Raising Achievement Group Meetings'

It is common practice in primary school for pupil progress meetings to take place. In secondary school there are often similar meetings and schools that are members of PiXL often include the words 'Raising Achievement' in the title for the meetings.

These meetings take place in conjunction with the collection of progress or tracking data. They may take place prior to data being finalised on the school system or take place following that point and will be led by Headteachers, senior or middle leaders.

In some schools they may take place every long term, every half-term and there are some schools who ensure such meetings take place more often such is their wish to accelerate progress. When meetings occur more often, new data is not collected on each occasion, instead the meetings focus on the skills the pupils are acquiring.

In essence the meetings look at which pupils are on track to meet their targets and what actions can be taken when a pupil is not on this trajectory so that by the next meeting they will have made an accelerated progress.

What can you do?

Ensure meetings are calendared and take place with the appropriate leader involved. In a one-form entry primary school, the Headteacher may choose to lead all Pupil progress meetings. Or the school may decide they wish to empower literacy and numeracy leads and in which case each teacher may have two shorter progress meetings with these colleagues. An alternative is if the structure is based around Key Stage leads and, in this case, they will lead their meetings. The Headteacher should have a meeting with the two leads. A school may decide to have more frequent meetings with key year groups such as year 2, year 6 and year 11.

In larger schools and secondary schools, it may be a Head of Department leads the meetings with their teachers and then senior leaders meet with the middle leaders. Again, the Headteacher should meet with senior leaders to prompt challenge.

It is important to decide if the meetings are scheduled to take place prior to data being finalised. In this scenario the meeting will begin with considering how accurate the data is thought to be with focus given to standardisation, perhaps including comparison with mock scores (Action 45). In other schools, leaders may be satisfied with the accuracy of date which has been inputted and in which case a deeper analysis of the data will be considered.

'Pupil progress meetings are most effective in a carefully considered structure'

Action 24:

Ensure pupil progress meetings focus on the skills that individual children need

In some schools, pupil progress meetings have not had the impact they should have and have also become very unpopular with teachers. This tends to occur when the meeting just considers data.

When this happens there will be lots of conversation of what percentage of children are on target and what percentage are not. The next part of the discussion may then lead into identifying the percentage for different groups of children. Finally, it will be collected together to look at the percentage of children on-track to make combined Reading Writing and Maths in a primary setting. In a secondary setting this may be around the basics or progress score for the subject.

What has been missing is conversation about individual children and the barriers they have to making more progress or the support the teacher may feel they need to help the pupils make this progress.

What can you do?

If you are not leading the meetings, provide suggested questions which means the discussion is not focussed on numbers but moves to pupils. Consider which pupils are at risk of not reaching their target and in which subjects. How far away from their target are they? Is this a recent occurrence or have the pupils been 'off target' for a period of time such as more than an academic year?

When data use in a school is not well developed, the conversation with teachers and leaders about off-target pupils can cause improvement, especially if the colleagues where not fully aware of the expectation for individual children and as result the expectation increases.

For schools where targets are part of common currency, the focus needs to be on what specific actions will bring about improvement or what are the specific gaps in learning which need to be filled.

Some schools will reduce to this one action or a single learning objective, which needs to be met for each child below target in each of their subjects. This is then communicated to all colleagues in the school and then when they are having conversations with this child, this may be touched upon. In one primary school there were large posters in the staff room with these single objectives for Reading, Writing and Maths. When an objective was met it was replaced with a new one.

'Pupil progress meeting must focus on actions to be take'

Action 25:

'Triangulating evidence'

The majority of schools have moved to a system where individual teachers are not graded, but judgements are still being made as to whether the teaching standards are being met. In the days of teacher grading, when leaders were asked how they graded teachers, it was continually surprising how many schools made their judgements on one-off lesson observations.

Many schools said that this was not their practice but during conversations when they were asked about the strengths or areas for improvement of teachers this would revert to what they had seen in those scheduled observations.

Yet when a wider range of indicators where considered, these did not knit together. Schools may have had a far rosier image of practice and this often occurred when teachers ensured children were well behaved or compliant but the challenge or pace was not there. They could also have a negative view if the colleague found being observed difficult or if the relationship between the observer and the teacher were not positive.

What can you do?

The most important action you can take is to ensure that information from different self-evaluation tools are drawn upon alongside traditional observations. You need to be asking yourself what do learning walks, book scrutiny and outcomes data suggest about the strengths of the teacher? You do have to be careful when assessing outcomes data and carefully consider how much impact this teacher will have had upon them.

You may also consider more anecdotal information from pupil voice or parent comments. However, ensure that these just ask a question to look at rather than providing an answer.

Then triangulate all these sources of information to consider what strengths are being seen in individual areas or across the piece. Remembering that some teachers may have weaknesses in a particular area, which they have learnt to overcome in different ways. The obvious example here is the inspirational teacher who really makes the pupils think and hence they retain knowledge but the books may be messy.

Develop your own method of recording this. Some schools have moved towards a 'Teacher on a page' document (TOAP), which captures information from varying activities. Each time a piece of monitoring takes place the leader will make brief notes on the TOAP to form a chronology. This triangulates the strengths of the teacher and the areas that they need to develop.

'Triangulation of evidence is reliable and depersonalises findings'

Action 26:

Group staff according to grade and determine when support is needed

There is still a debate as to whether colleagues should be graded using the four OFSTED grades or not. If they are graded it should be from a wide evidence base not a single observation. Whether you use OFSTED grades or not, as a leader you need to determine whether your colleagues are effective or not. Then most importantly you need to decide on the actions that you can take to try and improve them.

In most areas of the country there is a shortage of teachers. If colleagues are not proving effective, it is often better to try and improve them so that they can be effective in your school.

It is likely that you will expect different standards of performance from a colleague who is in their first year of teaching compared to colleagues who are on the upper pay spine or leadership.

What can you do?

Some schools will use matrix as an indicator of when they will begin support processes for their colleagues. If you use OFSTED grades it may look like this. The teacher's initials are then placed in the appropriate box for their teaching experience and teaching quality.

Figure 3.2: Matrix to show the expected link between teaching experience and teaching quality

	4	3c	3b	3a	2c	2b	2a	1c	1
Leadership							■	■	■
UPS							■	■	■
M6						■	■	■	
M5						■	■	■	
M4						■	■		
M3					■	■			
M2				■	■				
M1			■	■	■				

The OFSTED grades have been subdivided and mean the following:
2c: Teacher is generally good across but a few elements require improvement
2b: Teacher is securely good across their practice.
2a: Teacher is securely good and a few elements of their practice are outstanding

If you do not want to use OFSTED grades you can replace the word Good with Effective / Teacher Standards, Outstanding with Exceptional and RI / Inadequate with ineffective.

Figure 3.3: Matrix to show the expected link between teaching experience and the Teacher Standards

	I	I+	TS-	TS	TS+	E-	E
Leadership					■	■	■
UPS					■	■	■
M6				■	■	■	
M5				■	■	■	
M4				■	■		
M3			■	■	■		

In the above table, TS refers to meeting the Teacher Standards, E is exceptional and I is Ineffective.

TS+: Always meets the teacher standards and is occasionally exceptionally

TS: Meets the teacher standards

TS-: Usually meets the teacher standards but is occasionally ineffective.

Colleagues on M1 and M2 are not included as they would be following the Early Career Framework standards.

The shaded areas of the grid indicate what you expect of teachers. If their practice falls to the left of the shading, then you would begin some form of support process. Equally if their practice is to the right of the shaded boxes, then you could give colleagues double increment pay progression if this is in your pay policy.

'It is not about grading, it should be about supporting or rewarding'

Action 27:

Prioritise senior leaders to model effective teaching

If you have highlighted some colleagues whose teaching is not effective in certain areas, you can often find that this is because they are not always sure of what effective looks like. In some situations, ensuring that they are effective can be as simple as modelling that practice and providing a conversation as to how they can implement this in their teaching.

It is important that in such circumstances you act quickly, rather than letting the situation drag on. This does not have to be a formal process but instead can be informal with a low-key conversation suggesting that an element of practice needs a little more precision and that you would like them to see somebody else model it.

What can you do?

The colleagues on your staff who will have a little more flexibility in their timetable are likely to be your senior leaders. You may also find that colleagues prefer something to be modelled in their own classroom so that they can see the action working with their own pupils.

You could group your senior leaders into subject specialisms (primary or secondary), age range specialisms (Primary EYFS/KS1 and KS2) or certain skills (questioning, assessment, behaviour, use of ICT etc.).

Then when some modelling is required for a colleague, you deploy the appropriate leader to give the intervention.

Such approaches work best when it is acknowledged that nobody is perfect and this is not about blame culture. Instead it about working together so that all teachers are as effective as possible

'Quickly deploy the appropriate colleague to model the element of teaching'

Action 28:

Moving from monitoring to development

Many schools have extremely well-developed systems for monitoring and evaluating the quality of teaching and learning. They will carefully undertake lesson observations, learning walks, book scrutinies, pupil focus groups and pupil progress meetings. They will have an accurate picture of the strengths and weakness of the provision.

This is very useful information but on its own it will not improve practice in a school. In some situations, it can actually make a school go backwards if teachers are resenting the activities that are being done to them and if their confidence is being reduced.

What is really needed is to change the focus away from being all about monitoring and instead to answer the question 'how do we develop our staff?'

This is about making a change in culture so that the same level of meticulous planning goes from the monitoring to the development of teaching and learning.

What can you do?

This is a huge area of work so the notes in this action only skim the surface of this topic but hopefully you will gain some ideas of how to get started. The first thing to is to look at policies and stop thinking of 'monitoring and evaluation' but instead 'evaluation and development'. A starting point is to look at the policy and ensure there is an equal focus on development as evaluation.

When leader's complete evaluation, they should always ask the question, how will this be developed? What interventions are required to improve practice?

Ensure that more time is given to discussing development than evaluation. Then try and distil it down to the key action for development, which needs doing next. Sometimes we can over face ourselves with so many development points that actually nothing happens or improves.

'What is the one thing that will make the next improvement?'

4 RAISING EXTERNAL OUTCOMES

There will be occasions in a school leader or system leader's career when they just need to raise external outcomes as fast as they can. There are two reasons for this. The first and most important is the children. Their futures will be determined by their external outcomes. This is obvious at Key Stage 4 and Key Stage 5 where post 16, Higher Education and career choices are dependent on a child's grades. Whilst not being explicit at Key Stage 2, children will be grouped in some secondary schools according to their Key Stage 2 outcomes, and hence the result a child receives in year 6 can influence their starting trajectory towards their GCSE examinations.

Secondly, even with the latest OFSTED handbook there are some situations when external outcomes can limit the judgement a school receives and this is a judgement that can stay with the school for three and even four years. Even if you have implemented the most amazing curriculum, you need to have external outcomes at a certain level.

This chapter contains a set of twenty-four actions, which you can implement to gain some short-term impact on outcomes. If these are the only school improvement strategies that you undertake, you are unlikely to achieve long-term growth but they can help start the school moving in the right direction whilst you are also working on quality first teaching. Or they may provide that little extra that helps you polish already strong outcomes.

The following table allows you to track which actions you have implemented over the course of the academic year and the Key Stage they are most applicable to. The subtitle of the book is 'Day In, Day Out

Improvement', so it is suggested that you return to them on a term-by-term basis too and there is a column for each long term, which you can annotate.

At the end of year, you should ask yourself two questions:

- What has been the impact?
- What do we need to do differently to maintain / increase the impact?

Figure 4.1: Summary of actions to raise external outcomes

	Action	Primary	Secondary	T1	T2	T3
29	Ensure the gaps in last year's performance are being tackled	✶	✶			
30	Ensure the most effective teachers have significant contact with year 6 or year 11	✶	✶			
31	Ensure 'bands' have all ability pupils within them		✶			
32	Review targets so they are sufficiently challenging	✶	✶			
33	Analyse whether the curriculum is P8 compliant		✶			
34	Are guided options in place to ensure appropriate children study EBacc subjects?		✶			

35	Check GCSE equivalent courses are still compliant		✱		
36	Analyse if early entry for English Literature or Language is the best approach		✱		
37	Maximise learning time	✱			
38	Address weaknesses at the start of the school day	✱			
39	Check the phonics scheme is being used appropriately	✱			
40	Ensure the Maths scheme has a range of consolidation exercises	✱			
41	Ensure all children regularly practise Maths reasoning activities	✱			
42	Analyse the 'cross-over'	✱	✱		
43	Using 'war rooms'	✱	✱		
44	Study the intervention strategies being used	✱	✱		
45	Consider the accuracy of historical predictions	✱	✱		

46	Ensure that PiXL is being used appropriately	✸	✸			
47	Interventions outside of the school day	✸	✸			
48	Additional interventions in the school day	✸	✸			
49	Review long term planning	✸	✸			
50	Who are the vulnerable children?	✸	✸			
51	Promote a 'can do' culture	✸	✸			
52	Ensure practice tests match the real thing	✸	✸			

RAISING EXTERNAL OUTCOMES

THE ACTIONS

Action 29:

Ensure the gaps in last year's performance are being tackled

Depending on when you are working in the school you will have statistical historical analysis. If it is early in the autumn term you will not have official progress measures but you can compare how different groups of pupils are performing.

Studying overall attainment may not help you, as the cohort could be very able or have low starting points. Instead study the performance of different groups; Higher Prior Attaining, Middle Prior Attaining and Lower Prior Attaining pupils and see how their performance compares with national averages.

Later in the autumn term, when the ASP (Analyse School Performance) document and the IDSR (Inspection Dashboard) will have been released, you can look at progress measures for different subjects.

It is important to analyse the progress from one Key Stage to the next. It is not uncommon in a primary school to have very different progress from EYFS to Key Stage 1 in comparison to Key Stage 1 to Key Stage 2.

From this analysis you are trying to determine if particular groups of students or a subject area is underperforming.

What can you do?

You need to question what is being done to address the areas for involvement:

- Does the school have the skills within to make improvement, or do you need to seek help from an outside specialist such as an SLE to provide support and guidance?
- Is there an action plan with milestones which you can monitor to determine if improvements are being made and these gaps will reduce?

'If we do what we've always done, we will get what we always have.'

Action 30:

Ensure the most effective teachers have significant contact with year 6 or year 11

It is a fact of life that if you are quickly trying to improve a school, you need to rapidly improve the results of the year groups sitting external tests. In primary schools, a number of year groups receive external outcomes, yet it is still year 6 which is given the most focus.

In secondary schools, our first aim is always to improve year 11 outcomes. The most important reason is that for the children they only have one chance to take their GCSEs and the results affect the life chances of these pupils.

Even at KS2 this is important for the children. Many secondary schools will band their children according to their KS2 results and it is a sad fact that children will perform better the higher the set they are in. It is also true that it is always easier to stay in a higher set than to climb into one.

What can you do?

In secondary schools, school leaders often say 'of course our best teacher/s are working with year 11' to which a reply is 'but are they teaching as many children as they can?' If there are six forms in a year and the school has an outstanding English teacher, can the classes be split into two populations or bands so that the teacher has a class in each band.

Some schools find more creative solutions. A small secondary with four-form entry may have one specialist Science teacher and three non-specialists. Could the specialist teacher perform some large-scale teaching in the hall with three of the groups and two of the non-specialists supporting them? Finally, how are senior leaders supporting year 11 teaching?
In primary, when a specialist year 6 teacher leaves, this always leaves a hole

which is not always easy to plug. Leaders must think carefully about who is the best person to teach the group. It is not a case of who volunteers or who will complain the least. Again, a senior leader may be the solution but they might not be able to teach the class full-time. They could teach them each morning or four out of five mornings to ensure that they deliver the Reading, Writing and Maths.

It may be that the best teacher are senior leaders but do not have the capacity to teach a full class whilst maintaining their leadership role. In this case you may need to class share in a primary or in a secondary, split classes may enable strong teacher to have impact on a range of pupils.

'At this critical time, they deserve the best that we have got'

Action 31:

Ensure 'bands' have all ability pupils within them

Large secondary schools often split year groups into two populations of children. Schools with nine-form entry may even divide them into three populations.

What can happen is that schools may place their top sets in one band and their lower sets in another band. For example, a six-form entry school may have two top sets, three middle sets and a lower set. The school decides that two top sets and a middle set will go into one band and two middle sets and the lower set goes into another band.

On the surface this may work for the subjects, which teach in sets. However, those subjects who use mixed ability groupings have skewed sets and there may be half of the classes will not have any more able children in them.

It also means that children in two of the middle sets have logistical challenges if the teacher thinks they should be placed in a higher set and often this means that they do not get moved.

The biggest issue is that bands get labelled and once this happens, it is human nature that those children in the band with the more negative label are not given the same aspiration. There may also be more behaviour issues.

What can you do?

If you are banding children, try and form mixed ability populations and also look at other pupil groups such as gender and disadvantage and try and ensure these are equally distributed too.

'Don't put any glass ceilings on aspirations'

Action 32:

Review targets so they are sufficiently challenging

The biggest glass ceiling many schools place on their pupils is the targets they set them, whether this is at Year 11, Year 6 or even in early years when looking at which pupils can achieve a Good Level of Development (GLD).

One of the most powerful actions leaders can take is to increase the targets for children, alongside a supportive conversation of 'what can we all do to reach these targets.' It is often found that removing targets from appraisal and pay progression is important in building this culture.

It is sometimes the case that schools which are performing 'ok' but not making the improvement do not have aspirational targets. They could be unsure as to what are appropriate targets. In the past it was relatively straight forwards with three levels of progress in secondary and two levels of progress in primary: the standard all pupils should be attaining and four levels (secondary), three levels (primary) was better than expected progress. Life after levels has removed that easy comparison.

What can you do?

For this reason, it is often sensible to use Fisher Family Trust (FFT) targets: however, with three different parameters schools do not always choose the most appropriate. FFT50 targets place a school in the top 50% (the top half) of schools nationally. FFT20 targets place a school in the top 20% and FFT5 in the top 5%. One rule of thumb is that Outstanding schools or those on the cusp of outstanding should use FFT5. Good or aspiring to be good schools will use FFT20 and those trying to escape from a category may use FFT50.

However, you need to go a step further when you are setting targets for individual children. If you are using FFT20 and look at an individual child, you may actually think there is a chance they could get to FFT5 and if so set them this as an individual target. What you should try to avoid is reducing FFT20 targets for an individual child.

This system works equally well at year 6 as year 11. If you are looking at the youngest children, even in the most deprived setting you should be trying to reach national for GLD. In this scenario, when children are a long way from GLD on entry to the school. You have to ask the question what can we do to give children the best chance of reaching GLD and how can we implement this?

'Do not be concerned that you might set a target too high and fail. Be concerned that you will set it too low and succeed'
Michelangelo

Action 33:

Analyse whether the curriculum is P8 compliant

One question that all school leaders should be asking is what proportion of children in Key Stage 4 are studying a curriculum that will fill each of the eight slots for Progress 8. How many children are studying three subjects which are eligible for Bucket two, the EBacc qualifications and how many children have a further three open subjects?

You can find that if you are new to a school the curriculum does not achieve this due to the suite of options that are offered. This is becoming less common over time as leaders become more used to the P8 measurement.

What can still happen though, generally by accident rather than design, is that decisions are made for individual or small groups of students by looking at a single subject and the broader impact on P8 has not been considered.

What can you do?

Are all the subjects that are offered children Progress 8 compliant? Do they actually count? There may be some students who are following a specific pathway with subjects that are not P8 compliant: if so who are they? What proportion of the cohort are they? This is not to say that such courses should not be offered, as a school may make a careful decision that the qualification is in the best interests of certain children.

Check whether children have been allowed to drop courses by middle leaders. Has this information been shared with the senior leader who is responsible for academic standards? Have they calculated the impact that this will have on overall P8 figures?

For children who are not studying a P8 compliant curriculum it may be possible for them to study additional qualifications that make their curriculum compliant. This has been implemented for year 11 students where they use time in the day and outside of the traditional school day.

'Are the right buckets filled for the right children?'

Action 34:

Are guided options in place to ensure appropriate children study EBacc subjects?

The government still has an aspiration that a very significant proportion of students will study the EBacc suite of qualifications, i.e. will study Science, a Humanities subject and a Modern Foreign Language.

The original aspiration was all students; this is now 90% by 2025. The OFSTED handbook does state that 'Inspectors will not make a judgement about the quality of education based solely or primarily on its progress towards the EBacc ambition.'

What can you do?

School leaders have to decide how important the EBacc offer is to their students. Schools who believe all pupils should study the EBacc will have carefully designed their options process to ensure it happens. Students will choose between History and Geography, choose a Modern Foreign Language and then have two or possibly three further options.

There are schools that do not make the EBacc prescriptive. Instead children can choose to study the EBacc. If this approach is being taken, it may be wise to 'guide' the options process so groups of pupils do opt for the EBacc subject.

There are perhaps three main ways to achieve this.
1) A school may provide an options form for certain pupils where they have to select an EBacc offer.

2) A school may run an options evening where the EBacc is explained and heavily promoted to parents and pupils so that they are strongly encouraged to opt in this manner.

3) Pupils may have individual meetings with a teacher where they are encouraged to study an EBacc subject when it is felt it is appropriate for the child.

'When is an option not an option, when it is guided!'

Action 35:

Check GCSE equivalent courses are still compliant

Ofqual normally ensures that courses are given two years' notice as to whether they are compliant for school performance tables. This means that you know if a child starts to study a course in year 10 and it is compliant then it will also be compliant when they sit their GCSE examinations in year 11.

If pupils study a three-year Key Stage 4, they may opt for something that is compliant during their year 9 and year 10 studies but when they are examined at the end of year 11 the course is no longer compliant.

In the worst-case scenario schools have used an examination for all children and then found in year 11 that for all those children one of their A8 and P8 slots is not filled, which can have a huge impact on overall school figures.

It tends to be vocational subjects where there is movement around compliance i.e. subjects where the qualification obtained is not a GCSE but an equivalent qualification.

What can you do?

If you do use a three-year Key Stage 4 ensure that compliance is checked at the end of year 9. If the subject is deemed not compliant at this point, then you should be prepared to change the qualification for the course.

There are lists of compliant qualifications so it should be possible to find one that is similar and covers similar material to the original qualification and then change to that one.

Teachers may have to rewrite schemes of work and change some content but this is worth it in the end.

Similarly, if you study a two-year Key Stage 4 ensure that teachers check before the options process that their subject is still compliant and that they show leaders evidence of this. It is can be easy to miss a change like this if the qualification has been used over a long time period by the school.

'Check the qualification still counts and then check it again!'

Action 36:

Analyse if early entry for English Literature or Language is the best approach?

A number of schools have been entering their year 10 students for either the English Language or English Literature examination. They explain that this allows them to focus their teaching on one of the examinations in year 10 and then change their focus for the other examination in year 11.

There are those who believe it is better to do English Literature in year 10 and others that it is better to sit English Language in year 10. In addition, because either English course can be used for the 'Basics' and 'Bucket One' for A8 and P8, schools may say that is acceptable that the other qualification is lower as it will not count in this measure.

From a pupil perspective this may seem the wrong decision. It is often accepted that most children will perform less well in the year 10 qualification. This can have a negative impact on the self-esteem of the child whether their target is a 9 or a 3 as they perform lower and then believe they cannot do it. In addition, the child has a GCSE grade lower than they should have.

From a performance table perspective, the second English qualification may be important to the child in the open bucket. It is surprising how many children who study both English qualifications in year 11 have a higher grade in their second English qualification than in some of their other open bucket subjects.

Finally, there is also the question as to whether sitting one of the English qualifications in year 10 is actually 'gaming'? Is the school planning in the best interest of the child?

What can you do?

Analyse historic results from sitting English in year 10. Consider how the two results compare. Ask yourself is it in the best interest of the child to sit an English qualification in year 10? Or would they get higher grades by sitting them both in year 11?

'Get the highest grades in Literature and Language'

Action 37:

Maximise learning time

One of the big challenges that schools face is ensuring children have the time to cover the curriculum. In the past, leaders of many primary schools that were in challenging circumstances would reduce the breadth of the curriculum. The children would spend significant proportions of time working on their Reading, Writing and Mathematics. The result was that limited time would be given over to wider areas of the curriculum.

Most school leaders would not necessarily agree with this for philosophical reasons but such was the pressure to increase the results that they would feel as though they had little choice.

The new OFSTED framework has made this approach far more difficult with the greater emphasis being given to the whole curriculum. This means that school leaders need to think carefully as to how they can squeeze more out of the curriculum time.

What can you do?

In many schools, children will be allowed into classrooms 10 or 15minutes before formal learning starts. Perhaps if school days begin with registration at 8:45am, children will be allowed in the classroom at 8:30am. Typically this has been a time that teachers have encouraged children to read their class book.

In some schools this time has been named as the 'Start of Day Activity' time or S.O.D.A. time with the children being given a specific activity to work on in this time. It could be something related to learning that will take place that day. Some schools may consider some focussed pre-teach activities with a particular group of pupils. It could be a consolidation activity to reinforce learning or a task where children have to reflect on their learning from the day before.

Teachers who promote this activity can find that children then begin to be at school for this time and look forward to the SODA time. The result is that pupils can add an extra 15minutes of learning to the start of each day. This adds up 75minutes a week and over the course of the year that is 47.5hours or nine extra days of learning!

'Get the most out of your school day'

Action 38:

Address weaknesses at the start of the school day

In most primary schools there will be a key area of children's learning that is being worked upon across the school. It could be an issue that has been highlighted as an area for improvement from an OFSTED report, it could have been highlighted in a school review or it could be seen in a dip in the data.

There may be a weakness in handwriting, perhaps Maths KS2 results are low or there may be serious gaps in the reading ability of the children. In such a situation, address this as a whole school issue, something that every teacher and every teaching assistant is working upon.

To ensure this is highlighted as a whole school issue and is given the prominence it requires across the whole school, the school could decide to practise it at the beginning of each and every school day. It could be the 'Start of the day activity' (S.O.D.A.) for when the children are arriving in school prior to the register being taken, or it could be the first task that the children are completing after the register.

What can you do?

In a school where Maths was the low point in the data, the teachers agreed that every morning across the whole school during registration, all the children would be completing five Maths questions. This was in addition to their normal Maths lesson.

In another school, handwriting had been highlighted as an area for an improvement so as a SODA activity prior to the register: every class in the school was completing a task to support handwriting. For very young children this may have been looking at fine motor skills whereas as further up the school the children had a handwriting activity.

It does not have to be at the start of the day, it could also be an activity during afternoon registration. The real power is that it is an issue which is being addressed by the whole school at the same time.

'It's always best to solve problems together'

Action 39:

Check the phonics scheme is being used appropriately

Most primary schools will have purchased a phonics scheme, or chosen a phonics approach, which is used with their younger children. There are many different products available and teachers often feel very protective over the scheme they have chosen.

In some MATs, they use the same phonics scheme across all the schools in the Trust. In these circumstances when the change is implemented some teachers will be very positive about the scheme whereas other teachers will say it is not effective and children will not learn. This highlights that one phonics scheme is not necessarily better than another but the key is how it is used.

What can you do?

It is important that whichever phonics scheme is used, all teachers are trained in how to use it effectively and are then observed by a phonics specialist who can give feedback on how accurately it is being used.

When some leaders observe a teacher use a phonics scheme that the observer knows well, they often see that the teacher is mixing approaches from different schemes together. This may not be noticeable to someone without this specialism and the teaching may look acceptable but in this scenario the children will not make the progress that they should.

The best phonics delivery is often to smaller groups and one way of enabling this to happen is to make sure that teaching assistants are well-trained in the delivery of phonics. This allows you to create groups across different year groups and even Key Stages based on the phonics needs of individual children.

Pupils need to be placed in appropriate ability groups rather than age groups and some schools will have groups from varying classes and even across the Key Stage.

Schools need to ensure that the phonics scheme is being used appropriately and all staff receive expert training. Also ensure that the teaching is of phonics is observed by someone who knows the approach being used inside and out. In this way it can be checked that schemes are not being joined together. When schools think another scheme will give better outcomes, they should move to the new scheme.

It is important to ensure pupils have the opportunity to practise their phonics skills. One way of doing this is to provide children with two appropriate reading books, one that matches the phase learning and one which is a challenge.

'Use phonics schemes with fidelity'

Action 40:

Ensure the Maths scheme has a range of consolidation exercises

Many schools use a Maths scheme across their school whether it is *White Rose Maths* from a Maths hub or a commercial scheme with PowerPoints or textbooks. These are really useful for school leaders as they ensure progression as the children move through the schools and also give good coverage of the curriculum.

It is recognised that consolidation of skills is so important in Maths and this goes beyond the practice of timetables and mental methods, but children need a constant cycling of Maths techniques as they learn new ones, or they will find it hard to build their Mathematical skills.

Some commercial Maths schemes do not give many consolidation exercises, otherwise known as fluency practice. An inexperienced teacher, or one lacking confidence, can feel they are doing really well as they are keeping up with the scheme and the children are progressing on a day-by-day basis. They seem to know it at the time so on the tracking software being used, the objectives are constantly being 'Ragged' as green, 'objective met.' Yet when they come to an assessment (if these are done) the children do not seem to be able to recall the technique.

This does not mean the topic was not explained well at the time or even the pupils could not do it at the time but if the pupils do not have the opportunity to complete enough consolidation exercises the concept will not 'stick'.

What can I do?

Teacher should be encouraged to supplement the fluency exercises given in the scheme. Those given should be seen as the bare minimum and a guide to the type of questions that the child should be tackling rather than the entirety of the work. This should also mean the lesson has more pace as the teacher encourages the children to move through the material.

Consider Maths as cyclical: teachers should be encouraged to return to topics so the children have more opportunities to practise them. Certain Maths lessons could be put aside as consolidation lessons across the school to match a whole school timetable system.

In fluency time, encourage teachers to set written questions which act as consolidation of learning objectives in addition to mental methods. Pupils should also have daily opportunities to practise retrieval skills.

If Maths is a target area for a school, use the idea of Action 38 (Address weaknesses at the start of the day) so the children complete a number of consolidation exercises every day. This could be to recap the previous day's learning.

'Don't just practise the Maths once'

Action 41:

Ensure all children regularly practise Maths reasoning activities

Leaders often say to me, 'we've brought in a Maths scheme so we know that the children have covered all the material. The tracking tool has been used to show which children have met their objectives. We have also used a range of consolidation exercise. But still the children are not achieving what they should do'.

One element in this scenario is often the use of Maths reasoning activities. The pupils are not doing enough of them or more commonly not all pupils are being given the time to access them. Or sometimes they become a bolt-on such as 'problem solving Friday'.

There can still be a feeling that reasoning questions are a differentiation exercise for the more able. They are the 'tricky' questions that the pupils move onto when they have finished the consolidation exercise and as a result significant swathes of the class may not have the opportunity to apply their reasoning skills to Maths questions. Reasoning requires just as much practice as the actual Maths technique in fact more as it is often harder to apply something than just to practise it by rote.

What can you do?

First of all, ensure that there are reasoning skills of different difficulty available for all the children rather than them just being really tricky questions that only the most able children can answer. The root of reasoning questions is the 'why'. If a school is struggling to develop reasoning questions that are accessible for less able children, one solution is to take the reasoning questions provided to a younger year in the Maths scheme.

Some schools will print their reasoning questions on stickers, which the children then stick in their books. As a leader this makes it easier to monitor that all children are tackling reasoning questions. When a learning walk is being completed just pick up the books of low prior attaining children to check they have attempted the reasoning stickers in them.

Ensure that the reasoning is present in all lessons. There could be a whole school decision as to when reasoning takes place in the lesson. It could be at the beginning to practise skills from the previous day. It could be after 30minutes of the lesson that the children have 10minutes of reasoning before the plenary. Some schools decide that there is a specific slot in the timetable for a Maths reasoning lesson. When teachers are more confident in teaching reasoning a far more flexible approach should be used.

'It's not just rote learning, reasoning is vital too'

Action 42:

Analyse the 'cross-over'

One of the very powerful strategies that schools use to maximise the performance of year 6 children achieving Combined Reading, Writing and Mathematics or year 11 children achieving 'The Basics' is by carefully analysing the cross-over of these students.

Many schools like to give this a pictorial representation and Venn diagrams are one of the simplest diagrams that you can use. For year 6 it would be three circles and for the year 11 it would be two circles. You are looking for as many students as possible in the cross-over section and as a teaching team you can look at the children who are not in this section and consider what actions you can take so that they do move into that section.

Figure 4.2: Venn diagram for combined reading, writing and mathematics

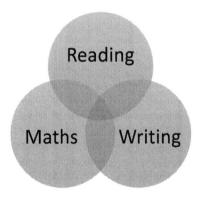

What can you do?

The first stage is to collect some performance data. Ask teachers to predict which children will meet the expected standard in Reading, Writing and Maths or which children will achieve a grade 5 in Maths and English. (For more thoughts on predictions, turn to Action 45).

This information is then used to construct a Venn diagram to show which children are achieving that 'cross-over'. Many tracking systems have a tool to produce these Venn diagrams from the data already inputted.

Leaders need to take some actions according to which children are not in the 'crossover. Many schools will consider which children require the least input so that they can achieve the crossover and begin work with these pupils first.

Finally keep monitoring the performance of the children as it is often fluid and pupils can move out of the crossover section.

'If a pupil can attain one subject how they can be supported to achieve the others'

Action 43:

Using 'war rooms'

As the number of pupils increases in a cohort it is more difficult to keep track of their performance and more importantly what actions individual children need to make to achieve their best.

School often find that it can be some of the quiet children who do not achieve their potential as they fly under the radar and it is just assumed that they are doing ok.

What can you do?

So, what is a 'war room'? Some schools have created displays in specific rooms using pictures of children so that they can analyse how they are performing. The simplest example would be the Venn diagrams from Action 42 with small photos of the children in addition to names. Some schools have created far more sophisticated displays.

In primary some schools may have separate displays for Reading, Writing and Maths. A child who is not achieving their crossover may have the key target that they need to work on for that week listed on the displays. When senior leaders are completing their monitoring, they can focus on individual children and ask them about their key target for the week.

In secondary, there may be a focus on progress 8. So, the P8 is completed for each child based on their predictions and then they are placed in groups according to their performance. Senior leaders can see which subjects they are underperforming on and can focus their learning walks by dropping into those individual subjects and provide some support.

GDPR legislation have made schools nervous over this approach so leaders need to ensure that these are in private areas and not locations where children, parents and other staff meet. For example, the displays may be in a senior leadership office and there will be blinds covering the displays. This room is used for the pupil progress meetings and SLT meetings so that staff are continually aware of the focus on outcomes.

The key to these types of strategies is that there must be actions following the analysis or the performance will not change.

'Use displays to individualise whole school performance figures'

Action 44:

Study the intervention strategies being used

It is very common for a range of intervention strategies to be used to raise the performance of pupils. There are the fluid interventions that occur during the lesson and those that take place at other times. It is often assumed that these second intervention strategies are actually taking place and that those used are of a good quality. It is important that a member of staff checks to see that this is the case.

What can you do?

The first thing to look at is who is doing the interventions. Again, it is easy for the teacher to say that the teaching assistant is working on interventions whilst they are teaching the whole class. The flaw in this is that interventions are with pupils who have not achieved the first time.

Therefore, it should be the most skilled practitioner who is then working to address these gaps.

Secondly which materials are being used for the interventions? They require high quality materials if they are going to help children achieve more than they did the first time of teaching. Someone needs to be looking at the materials to check this is the case.

It is also important to look at what is being covered. If interventions are catch-ups from the material of the week, this is relatively straightforward. If the interventions are at the end of the course and in the final run-up to assessment, it is important that the material is carefully thought through. This could be by studying practice or mock papers and addressing those gaps or it could be by looking at examiners' reports and covering the gaps.

Senior leaders should encourage their staff to publish their planning. In secondary schools you may have the intervention foci as a poster so both children and staff can see what is being covered. In primary schools it could be a notice to staff and parents.

Some schools will create an intervention map showing the range of actions being implemented with different children. They may also produce personalised action plans.

Finally look at when interventions are being completed. In primary if they are being completed during lesson time, what are children missing out on as a result? What impact are they having on the overall curriculum that is being covered? In secondary, ensure there is a timetable to try and avoid clashes, use options blocks to try and minimise this happening.

'The most effective interventions are carefully planned and timely'

Action 45:

Consider the accuracy of historical predictions

Most secondary schools will ask middle leaders for predictions at points in the year. In the past this may have only been at two points, once following mocks and then just prior to examinations. With the growth of in-school tracking this increased and it was not uncommon for this to be a half-termly process. One school completed them on a fortnightly basis! With concerns over workload, predictions have decreased and possibly three or four sets of predictions would be normal.

Primary schools have followed this process particularly if they are in Multi Academy Trusts consisting of primary and secondary schools. Though sometimes it is found that primary teachers are less confident in using predictions.

If predictions are going to be used inform interventions, they need to be accurate. Otherwise you will be intervening with the wrong students. Therefore, it is important to look back to last year's data and compare the final results achieved by the pupils with the predictions that the teachers made prior to assessment and consider how accurate they were.

What can you do?

Schools can implement processes which aim to improve the quality of predictions. For example, in primary, schools could have two sets of mock tests using the previous two years of SATs papers with a guide as to where children should be if they are going to make the expected standard or greater depth.

The following table shows a trajectory to reach both the expected standard and greater depth.

Figure 4.3: A trajectory model for expected standard and greater depth

		November Mock	February Mock	Final Results
ARE	Standardised Score	95	98	100
GDS	Standardised Score	105	108	110

In secondary schools a similar process can be used. Schools can create their own trajectories to use for predictions. One flight path could be that pupils would be expected to improve by half a grade from mock to the final exam and for greater improvement, more intensive interventions will be required. This could be converted to UMS scores for each exam for a more forensic method.

The table below shows the trajectory of pupils improving by a complete grade from their year 10 examination for the OCR Maths exam at the foundation tier.

Figure 4.4: A trajectory model for GCSE UMS

		Year 10 Mock	November Mock Nov	February Mock March	Final Results
Grade 5	UMS Foundation Papers	139	152	164	176
Grade 4	UMS Foundation Papers	102	115	127	139

It can be very complicated to use trajectories for GCSE using UMS scores as different subjects and different exam boards will calibrate them differently.

You could also deploy Specialist Leaders of Education or experienced moderators to work with teachers in lessons to see if they feel that the children are working at the level which the teacher is predicting.

'Accurate data tracking will ensure accurate interventions'

Action 46:

Ensure 'PiXL' is being used appropriately

The previous four actions will no doubt have resonated with those school leaders who have or currently subscribe to the PIXL network, whether in primary, secondary or post 16.

PIXL or the Partners in Excellence is a national network of schools that via conferences and school visits shares strategies to improve outcomes in their schools. In the past this focused on interventions to support attainment but now there is a growing focus on pastoral support.

Many school leaders have strong feelings about PIXL: both positive and negative. Some school leaders believe that PIXL is a key part of their school's success whereas other school leaders consider it to be a wasteful use of money, which takes people away from focussing on quality first teaching.

If you are a PIXL subscriber, if you don't use it appropriately, it will be a waste of money and can even reduce standards.

What can you do?

Many people think PIXL is all about the conferences and whilst these are usually hugely informative, there is little point in attending the conferences if some of the actions discussed are not then implemented in school.

Through your PIXL subscription, you will have access to associate visits. The first thing you need to do is share what you did last year with the associate and ask for advice on how to make improvements and use these ideas.

If there are tests where you can download results, then use this process. If they suggest using grading in a certain way, then follow the procedure. If intervention strategies are suggested make use of them. As with action 44, think carefully as to who is the best person to deliver the interventions. One advantage of using PIXL is that you should have quality intervention materials to use.

Whenever you take on a strategy whether it is a primary school using a certain phonics package, or a post 16 institution using PIXL, if you half-heartedly implement it, you will not gain the outcomes that schools who really focus on it do.

'Use PIXL with fidelity'

Action 47:

Interventions outside of the school day

Schools that are trying to raise the performance of the children are always looking for opportunities to give children additional input beyond lesson time. They will look flexibly at the school day and see if there are moments when they can plan and run some additional teaching.

If this is not included in 1265 calculation of directed time, schools can only ask if teachers are willing to volunteer although many will if they see it as valuable. The Senior Leadership Team can be requested to take part. There may be also be non-teaching staff or volunteers who would also be involved.

Learning that takes place outside of the school day must also interest or be sold to the children. They will not necessarily come for more of the same unless their parents insist that they do so.

What can you do?

Firstly, look at using time before school. Breakfast clubs are often popular as children are often keen for some hot food before the school day starts. These are very common in the immediate run up to exams but some schools will extend them into the academic year.

In a previous section, action 37, SODA time for primary schools was explained. If there are children that regularly arrive in school early, could planned activities be run? A suite of computers could be used for an intervention such as 'Timetable Rock Stars' in primary to 'GCSE Pod' in secondary. This could also be an opportunity for children to read to adults if there are volunteers who like an early start.

Another strategy is to organise pre-teaching of the topic in the day ahead with a focussed group of pupils. A traditional revision lesson, which has been planned and communicated to children (and/or parents) with the topic that is being covered could also be delivered.

All of these ideas can also be used at lunchtime and in the after-school slot but what is important is that a schedule of what is being completed, and when, is planned. Have a range of adults providing the intervention. You could also employ additional teachers using pupil premium funding. This could also take place during the school holidays through a 'Summer School' or 'Easter School.'

'Be creative in using time outside the school day'

Action 48:

Additional interventions in the school day

It can be hard to involve children in interventions outside of the school day. Children may preciously guard their lunch times and after school slots for a whole host of reasons: from buses to parent choice, it may be hard to use time before school. This means we have to be creative in whether we can use time within the school day for additional interventions.

What can you do?

In secondary schools, tutor group time is often a good slot to use. Many schools will deploy a Maths and an English teacher as year 11 tutors. They will have small tutor groups made up of either key marginal Maths or English students and in this time they complete revision or fluency tasks. Other schools will decide that each day of the week has a different core subject focus and the subject staff will prepare materials that tutors will deliver with their pupils.

Some schools will look at what subjects they can free up. For example, they may reduce PE in year 11 and have materials, which students can study in this time. This needs to be managed carefully as some pupils will greatly resent losing their PE time to complete what they see as additional study. In primary schools it has been typical for other subjects to be squeezed out of the timetable to provide more intervention time for Reading, Writing and Maths. This is something which the new OFSTED framework is placing pressure on.

With careful teamwork between teaching assistant and teacher there may be some opportunities for intervention whilst keeping a rich timetable. For example, in some of the afternoon slots the teaching assistant could deliver the lesson and the teacher move individual or small groups of pupils and give short 'fluid' interventions to address misconceptions from the morning's learning.

In some schools when a times-tables practice is completed after the Maths lesson, the teacher could mark the Maths exercise whilst the teaching assistant delivers the times-tables test. The teacher can immediately address misconceptions whilst other pupils are completing a challenge activity.

Again, it is important to carefully timetable and plan how you are delivering the interventions. How can you deploy a range of adults to support the process so it does not just fall to the class teacher and class teaching assistant?

'Flex your school day to support intervention'

Action 49:

Review long term planning

Every year it is vital that all teachers review their long-term planning and ensure that full coverage of the curriculum is given. This review should be shared with senior leaders to double check the process, with the teacher talking the senior leader through their plans and the comparison with National Curriculum and the examinations syllabus.

This conversation should also link with both the school's intent, and the intent for the subject area. What is trying to be achieved through teaching this subject? Senior leaders should also be asking why the long-term planning is sequenced in a particular order and whether there are links to other areas of the curriculum.

What can you do?

The first stage, described above is the discussion of the comparison between the long-term planning and the published curriculum. In secondary it is important that the school leader asks the teacher to show them this in relation to the syllabus.

Every year there are teachers who deliver the wrong material or even the wrong syllabus because this check has not been done. This can have disastrous implications for pupils and schools. Senior leaders must never assume that teachers will be getting it right, as the implications of such mistakes can be catastrophic. So double check that assessment deadlines are in place with appropriate 'wriggle room'.

Ask the teacher to make comparison to their analysis of pupils' performance. Looking at either internal or external assessments, what did pupils struggle with last year and how is this being addressed this year. For example, in KS2 Maths it is surprising how much the SATS test is based on year 3, 4 and 5 material so how is this being revisited through the long-term planning? Colleagues who work across schools will be able to name schools whose outcomes have plummeted because they have ploughed on with year 6 materials without providing the recap of material in earlier years.

If you are using a commercial scheme, you need to check that the teacher has planned how they will work through this during the year. Has the teacher changed the order of delivery and if so why have they done this? Have other teachers done similar things?

Finally, keep all long-term planning in a similar format with agreed referencing between plans and the curriculum / syllabus. This will enable conversations to be more accurate as any anomalies will be easier to spot.

'Never assume long term planning has been completed and is accurate, always check'

Action 50:

Who are the vulnerable children?

This comes under the category of never assume anything. You need to constantly check that all the staff know who the vulnerable children are in your school.

There will be children in your school who are vulnerable for different reasons. This does not necessarily mean children who are 'pupil premium'. There will be pupils with medical needs, which make them vulnerable. Remind staff every term of this, as teachers will forget, especially in a large secondary school. There is a temptation to just remember those you teach until you meet that child with an acute medical need and you are on lunchtime duty, something happens and you weren't aware.

Then think about children who are vulnerable in terms of their outcomes. This could be the traditional groups that are in the IDSR or the ASP. Who are the disadvantaged children, the EAL children and the SEN children? There will also be pupils who had prior attainment who have not kept pace with their earlier trajectory of learning for a whole host of reasons. Just as important: Who are the children who are at risk of not achieving their target grades but are not part of the groups that you would find in DfE lists?

What can you do?

Some schools will ensure that books have discrete labels for children who are PP, EAL, SEN and other key groups in your school. This makes teachers constantly aware whilst they teach and assess the work of children who are traditionally vulnerable.

Ensure there are opportunities for regular conversations about the academic performance of children which includes minutes of responses with regard to vulnerable children. This could be during pupil progress meetings, line management meetings, middle leaders' meetings, subject meetings and senior leadership meetings.

Many schools will have displays in the staff room of specific pupils to watch out for.

Ensure that once a term, pupils with medical needs are highlighted to the staff with pictures. It is so easy to just assume that everyone knows until something dreadful happens.

'Who are the vulnerable children in your school?'

Action 51:

Promote a 'can do' culture

When this section was first planned, the action was 'promote a no excuse culture' but straight away this sounds pejorative so it has been changed to the positive affirmation of a 'can do culture'. In terms of outcomes what does this mean?

As a leader you have to move away from perspectives of colleagues that this child can't achieve this, or that child can't do it, but instead continually turn it around so that the conversation is 'What can you do?'

It does not mean that you are saying that every child will achieve their targets but what can we do to give them their best chance to meet or exceed their target grades?

What can you do?

In some primary schools when children first join the school, leaders begin with the perspective that every child will achieve the expected standard at the end of year 6 and every conversation and action in the school is focussed on what can we do to ensure the children are on this trajectory.

The same happens in secondary schools, when children join the schools in year 7 they look at the FFT5 targets and begin with the intention that every child will achieve this target. The question is then what action does the school take to ensure this is the case?

If you have moved into a school and you are working with year 11 or year 6 and you are trying to bring rapid improvement after children have received less than good teaching for a number of years, it is not as easy to say that all children will achieve these standards. In fact, if you do, you can run the risk of losing teachers so you may need to take a slightly different tactic. Begin with looking at what the current trajectory is. That is your base line, which achievement will not fall below. Then begin positive conversations around what can we do next to achieve certain steps.

1) What can we do to make sure that we achieve FFT50 targets?
2) Once we've done this what can do to achieve FFT20 targets?
3) Once we've done this, what can we do to achieve…

You may use different stepping-stones depending on how you measure performance. E.g., if you are in a primary school currently looking at 14 out of 30 on target for the expected standard. To achieve national average of around 66%, 20 children need to make Combined Reading Writing and Maths (CRWM). So, the conversation could be which are the next closest children, what do we need to do there? Then look at the next two children and have the same positive conversation before looking at the next two students and having that positive conversation.

With all colleagues, the conversation must always revolve around the same positivity, what can we do to get there?

'No excuses, no blame, just what can we do…'

Action 52:

Ensure practice tests match the real thing

Most schools will do some kind of practice tests for year 6 and year 11 students. In many primary schools they will complete one set of practice tests in the second half term of autumn and then another set of practice tests during the spring term.

In secondary schools, the number and duration of year 11 examinations generally means that a school will only complete one set of practice tests for all subjects. Increasingly though secondary schools are completing a second set of practice for Maths and English in the spring term.

These practice tests link with a number of previous actions, in that they are key in accurately targeting your interventions in so many ways. However, they can be misleading if not used carefully.

In one particularly vulnerable school with attainment figures in the teens, the school was on a rapid improvement trajectory. Practice tests, which had been marked by independent markers, also showed this to be the case. However, when the pupils came to sit the actual examinations, suddenly their lack of resilience kicked in and when they became stuck they were not able to keep going. The attainment was much lower than had been expected.

School leaders realised that even though they had done practice tests and teachers had followed regulations in them, the actual test environment had not been the same, from the classroom, the arrangement of desks, the invigilators and the readers and scribes. The children's practices had been too far removed from the real experience.

What can you do?

When you are organising practice tests try and ensure that they match the experience as closely as possible. Think about who will invigilate, who will scribe and prompt the real ones and try and utilise them for your practices.

Which rooms do you use with which pupils in them? Can you then use those rooms for the practices too?

How do you brief children prior to the examinations? Can you use the same processes for the practice test?

All the time you are trying to balance using the same systems without bringing too much disruption to the rest of your school.

'Make practice as close as practicable to the real thing'

5 IMPROVING BEHAVIOUR

All school staff recognise that one of the hardest things to get right in a school is the behaviour of children. The context of a school does play a part in the behaviour of children and what is classed as good behaviour may vary from school to school.

If we can get behaviour right it has a huge impact on everything else that is done in the school and on all the colleagues within it.

There are lots of controversial actions which can be taken in schools. In 2019 there was considerable disapproval over a technique used by one Multi Academy Trust called 'Flattening the grass'. The academy Trust explained this was a method to 'create a level playing field by replacing the old systems that failed children. You have to flatten the grass – the bad practices – to pave a new way, a new vision.' In comparison an anonymous blog claimed children were the "grass" to be "flattened." There was considerable debate over what was really happening in these schools. Some leaders saw it as unacceptable whereas others saw it as an essential to the school improvement process. In 2020 there was also a growing campaign against using pupil isolation as a method of pupil behaviour management.

This chapter does not stray into such areas and each school leader will make up their own mind as to the appropriateness of such methods. Instead the actions that are listed in this section are the very basics of behaviour management. Many leaders will agree that in the vast majority of schools, if you can ensure these basics are in place and are used consistently day after day, you can make huge improvements in behaviour.

As with the other actions it as advised that you keep track of the actions that you implement over the course of the year and keep returning to them so they become ingrained practices. The majority are equally suitable for primary and secondary schools.

Following your implementation keep asking the key questions:

- What has been the impact?
- What do we need to do differently to maintain / increase the impact?

Good behaviour does not just happen; it takes lots of hard work by everybody in the school.

Figure 5.1: Summary of actions to improve behaviour

	Action	Primary	Secondary	T1	T2	T3
53	Visible presence at the start of the day from leaders	*	*			
54	Develop and implement a uniform sprint	*	*			
55	Ensure there is a clear and simple rewards system that the pupils buy into	*	*			
56	Introduce clear behaviour systems with consequences	*	*			
57	Are there rewards or treats for the always good?	*	*			
58	Ensure behaviour systems are followed by all	*	*			

	colleagues					
59	Ensure senior leaders have presence during the school day	*	*			
60	Set standards with year 11 and year 6	*	*			
61	Check that form time is used to support behaviour for learning	*	*			
62	Implement an exit process for pupils who are not following expectations	*	*			
63	Analyse where the most behaviour infractions are occurring	*	*			
64	Clear systems for managing break and lunch-time behaviour monitoring	*	*			
65	What is your alternative to exclusion process to provide breathing space between detentions and exclusions?	*				
66	Teachers take responsibility for managing behaviour in lessons	*				
67	Conduct a pupil focus group to ensure that the pupil view of behaviour	*				

	matches that of leaders					
68	Tidy up! Smarten up! Check the learning environment supports good behaviour	*				

5 IMPROVING BEHAVIOUR

THE ACTIONS

Action 53:

Having a visible presence at the start of the day

This is something that primary schools are generally very good at. It is common practice that the Headteacher and senior leaders will be on the playground at the beginning of the school day, welcoming pupils into the school and greeting parents.

Whilst these leaders will deal with some tricky issues at this point, so many smaller concerns can also be 'nipped in the bud'. Headteachers will need to explain to parents which member of staff will deal with the issues that are raised. If Heads do not do this they can find that pastoral issues could dominate their work every day.

This is not a regular action for Headteachers of secondary schools and it is unlikely that many parents would be greeted if they did. However, this simple act can have a huge impact on the children. It makes a statement that the people in charge of the school are not locked away from the children. If a school has got a significant breakdown in behaviour, this is a vital first action.

What can you do?

Many Heads and senior leaders will not meet and greet pupils due to staff briefing taking place in a morning so this may require moving to another time in the day.

Next consider which entrance most children walk through. It could be an entrance into the school grounds or the actual building itself. Then on a Monday morning wait for the pupils and greet as many pupils with a cheery 'good morning.'

Some schools will use this as an opportunity to deal with uniform issues, so that the children are dressed for school the moment they cross the threshold. Other school leaders will take a softly, softly approach of 'Good morning, oh and can you make sure you sort your…. Before you go into your form room'. The school should agree which approach they are taking amongst their leadership team.

Make it a routine and stick to it. Schools may decide to have a rota of who does the greeting. They may also do the same at the end of the school day.

'Build your relationships at the school gate'

Action 54:

Develop and implement a uniform sprint

Most UK schools have uniform and different leaders will explain a range of reasons for its importance from a group identity to ensuring that everyone is equal in the school. It tends to be true that one of the obvious signs of breakdown of behaviour in a school is when the uniform has little consistency. This lack of consistency is either due to teachers and leaders not feeling confident in tackling the issue and of the pupils (and the community) showing a lack of respect towards the school.

Improving uniform needs to be worked on by everyone in the school. It also should be done with little confrontation but by assertively asking pupils to do something. The most obvious route to confrontation is when pupils feel the system is unfair and different pupils are allowed to wear different things.

A 'sprint' is part of a project management system based on the idea of 'sprints, fixes and builds'. The idea of a sprint is that all members of the organisation focus on a topic at the same time and work towards it. The best sprints will be sub-divided so that everyone works on an action, then they move onto the next action and so on.

A sprint can be used to improve the quality of uniform in a school by looking at what good uniform will look like and then working on a plan so that this is achieved in a short but manageable time scale, rather than tackling everything on the same day.

What can you do?

If this is being read during the year and there is a feeling that behaviour has slipped, then leaders and teachers can plan a sprint of what they tackle each week together. There is far greater power when everybody is working on the same small action together rather colleagues trying to do everything at once.

Figure 5.1: A uniform sprint.

Week	Sprint Action
0	Prior to holidays use every method of communication available to the school to explain to parents and children what the expected uniform is with specific instructions of where it can be bought. One letter to parents will not suffice
1	Focus on skirts and trousers. Bring children together each day with a reminder of what is permitted and where it can be bought. Have a time limit of when it must be completed by. Schools will deal with this differently and every year there is a story in the newspapers about children not being allowed in school because of uniform depending on the school's severity of approach.
2	Jewellery: At the start of each lesson, staff to remind pupils of what is expected. Leaders must support staff with children who are likely to be an issue before it escalates.
3	Make-up: Same system as for jewellery.
4	Coats and hoodies: Same system as jewellery
5	Ties being worn correctly and sleeves not being rolled up: Same system as jewellery.
6	Celebrate the improvement that has happened.

Some people will say that this is too long a time scale but part of the length of time is about building habits. If something is tackled every day for a week, then a habit of good uniform will begin to be created.

It is also about the system being manageable and everybody having a sole focus. It can be found that if every uniform infraction is suddenly being challenged, then some staff can give up before the good habits are formed.

'Working together will form good habits'

Action 55:

Ensure there is a clear and simple rewards system that pupils buy into

Many people feel that some schools have a very elaborate systems of managing pupil behaviour but the same thought has not gone into the rewards system. Similarly, a reward system can quickly fall into disuse or only be used by a few members of staff. Equally the pupils may not value the reward system in place. In some schools, there have even been situations where pupils will choose to misbehave on occasions to avoid the reward system that is in use.

There are so many different reward systems whether they rely on stamps or written points to electronic systems via management information systems. There are also many outcomes ranging from 'Vivo' points where the children can buy things to certificates to badges to tickets in end of term raffles.

What can you do?

Ensure that all staff understand the reward system and encourage them to use it to reward all pupils and not just certain classes or certain groups of pupils. Have a target that teachers have to distribute so many rewards during the week.

Make sure the system is not labour intensive for teachers so this does not become a hurdle to children receiving rewards from a teacher.

Ensure rewards are in reach for all pupils. If the house points are being added up for a bigger reward, look at how long it is taking pupils to achieve them and whether they give up.

Communicate the rewards system to all and ensure that in each classroom there is a clear and simple explanation of the reward scheme so that everyone understands it.

Talk to pupils and check that there are no hidden disincentives, which demotivates the pupils. This could be as simple as the way that rewards are given out. Not all children wish for large-scale public recognition.

'Rewards should always come before sanctions'

Action 56:

Introduce clear behaviour systems with consequences

All schools will have a behaviour system. They often develop over time and will have responded to trends in behaviour at certain historical points and also possibly to the behaviours of certain groups of pupils.

As a result, behaviour systems can grow 'like Topsey.' By this it is meant that systems grow organically and sometimes in an uncontrolled fashion without a clear structure. They can become over complicated with a huge range of rules, covering every misdemeanour that can be thought of with just as large a group of consequences for each action.

Some colleagues will say that the one thing that ineffective schools have in common is a vast array of systems to punish pupils and staff!

Behaviour systems should serve a simple purpose to ensure that the school community is kept safe at all times and ensure that all children can learn in classrooms which are not being disrupted by others.

What can you do?

Review the rules that are in place. Can you reduce the number and simplify them? Can you reword them so that they become positive actions rather than a list of things not to do?

Consider the sanctions that are used: are they easily understood and straightforward to apply? Are there any unintended consequences that might mean sanctions actually result in rewarding pupils?

The result should be that the behaviour system can be captured on a single side of A4 paper and then displayed in every classroom. Pupils are then very clear as to what happens at certain points and staff can apply them very clearly.

If any more detail is required then this should be placed in the behaviour policy. Again, look for clarity and simplicity. Some schools have behaviour policies which are extremely long, which rather than clarifying expectation cause confusions for staff, pupils and parents.

"Clearly communicated and simple behaviour systems are the most effective"

Action 57:

Are there rewards or treats for the always good?

Often the biggest group of children in school are those who are always compliant. Within this group there are often two sets of pupils. There are those who gain good marks and consistently produce high quality work.

Then there are a second group of pupils who may not always shine in the quality of classwork.

The danger is that all these children can be forgotten and are often not rewarded. The children who are trying really hard are sometimes not rewarded because the teacher begins to always expect high standards from them and as a result can forget the effort and time that has gone into those pieces of work and homework. Those children who are not the high flyers can also be forgotten as they may be in classes with pupils who struggle to behave and the teacher will be focussing their attention on dealing with misbehaviour from the more vocal few.

What can you do?

Firstly, look for methods for rewarding pupils for their basic adherence to the school rules. Some primary schools have 'always' wristbands or badges that are given to pupils at the start of the half term, which they keep whilst they are always following the school expectations. In other schools children who have not received any behaviour points or incident entries over the half term receive a certificate or post card home to show that they have followed the expectations over the half term.

Some schools will have rewards trips or treats for those pupils who are always compliant. This could be as simple as a ticket to be able to go to the front of the lunch queue one day. In other schools it may be a trip to a local cinema, ten-pin bowling or theme park at a certain point in the year.

For those pupils who are really giving of their best, leaders need to encourage teachers to ensure that they are still praised and told how hard they are working.

In all situations, colleagues need to be aware of the law of unintended consequences and that the 'reward' is not seen as a reward, by the pupils. In one secondary school pupils were given an 'always good' certificate in a year group assembly. The result was that some of the older pupils would make sure they did one thing wrong just to ensure that they did not have to collect a certificate in front of their peers. Simply posting the certificate home to parents could easily overcome this issue.

'Ensure the reward is valued by the children'

Action 58:

Ensure all colleagues follow behaviour systems

Leaders will often say, behind closed doors, that if colleagues just used the behaviour system consistently, then the behaviour of children would rapidly improve. When leaders conduct pupil focus groups and ask questions about behavioural issues, pupils will often comment on perceived unfairness of various teachers using the behaviour system in different ways.

There will always be some level of inconsistency in how teachers respond to the behaviours of children, as everyone is an individual and have different thresholds of acceptance. Leaders need to ensure that when teachers respond they use the system. If a behaviour point means a teacher takes a certain action, leaders need to try to ensure that the action is taken.

What can you do?

Leading by example is key. Does your leadership team follow the behavioural system or are they doing their own thing? Are they completing the notes on the system, if it is electronic or filling in incident slips? If leaders are not doing this, other staff soon see. If leaders are not using the system because of the time it takes, then it will not be a surprise if other staff are doing the same.

Some leaders will refuse to support a member of staff if they system has not been followed. This is a tricky approach to take and can have negative consequences.

Some leadership experts have said that for colleagues to choose to follow a system, there are four aspects to look at. Is the action easy, timely, attractive and social? Easy is an obvious thing so if the system is complicated and takes too long, staff will not use it. Timely is around whether the system fits in with the working day. Attractive is linked to whether the system is seen to be effective. Finally, social, this is the power of the team; if everyone is seen to be using the system then people will be more likely to use it. The reverse of this could be that if staff become isolated by using the system, think of out of lesson detentions, they may be less likely to use them.

Consistent use of a system takes time and is a microcosm of the title of this book, staff must be encouraged every day to use the system and it must not be taken for granted.

'Consistency takes time and effort by all'

Action 59:

Ensure senior leaders have presence during the school day

There are two little tricks for managing pupil behaviour, which are always worth remembering and reflecting on. They are very simple.

The first is that teachers will manage behaviour more effectively if they feel confident and for many teachers a lack of confidence can be directly linked to a feeling of isolation and an anxiety that there is no-one there to 'back them up'.

The second is that pupils will often behave better if they feel that a number of people are checking in on them and that they are not just faced with one teacher on their own.

It is also found that pupils respond to hierarchy. Pupils will instinctively behave very differently for the Headteacher or a well-known senior leader.

This is not to say that the pupils do not behave well for colleagues at different levels of the hierarchy but those teachers will have had to work harder on this at some point.

What can you do?

It is important that when senior leaders are not teaching they have visible presence during the school day so that teachers feel supported in their lesson-by-lesson endeavours and so pupils feel a wide group of people are checking in on them.

In some schools, particularly those where they are trying to improve behaviour rapidly, there may be a decree that senior leaders never sit in their offices alone during the school day. Instead they are either teaching, working with teachers or walking the classrooms and corridors to support teachers managing the pupils.

In other schools, there may be a timetable so that for each lesson there is a senior leader on duty and they spend that lesson trying to drop in to as many lessons as possible, preferably to 'catch pupils being good' or otherwise support teachers with any issues that they may have.

The same should also be true at break and lunch times. The school may have all senior leaders on duty during these times. Or assign a duty manager who is checking in on all the teachers doing their duties.

'Senior leaders must be visible to support teachers'

Action 60:

Set standards with year 11 and year 6

In any school it is likely that younger pupils will first look to the oldest pupils to see how they are behaving and to a certain extent will then base their standards on what they see.

From an outcomes point of view, it is crucial that a school achieves high standards of learning behaviour from the oldest pupils as it will only be months before they sit their external assessments. Every learning moment really does count with these children and they cannot afford to waste learning time due to either their own behaviour issues or through being disrupted by other children in their groups and classes.

Finally, it is sometimes found that if teachers are nervous about dealing with behaviour of pupils it will be often be with the oldest children in the school. If you are a new or young teacher in a school, or both, then it can be human nature that a group of year 11's can be a little intimidating. There are some primary colleagues who say the same about year 6 children too.

What can you do?

This action builds on the previous section of visible senior staff supporting their colleagues.

Firstly, use assemblies and other opportunities to set standards and expectations for these year groups. External assessments should not be used as a threat to try and scare pupils into behaving as this is unlikely to work for any time nor is it conducive to building the confidence of children as they face these challenges. Instead senior staff could explain how they are the most important pupils in the school that year.

At the start of the new year, ensure that senior leaders are regularly dropping into year 6 and year 11 classes so that these year groups quickly realise that there is a focus on their learning.

Ensure the locations of year 11 lessons are clearly marked so that those on patrol ensure they check in on the lessons.

This is particularly important at the beginning of each lesson. Older pupils by their nature are larger and school buildings are often short of space particularly in communal areas outside classrooms. So, ensuring there are senior leaders available so that the start of lessons is smooth can be very effective. It also means that teachers can quickly get into their teaching stride.

'Visibly support the learning of year 6 and year 11'

Action 61:

Check form time is used to support behaviour for learning

When the signal is made to begin the start of a school day in the vast majority of secondary schools, pupils will troop towards their form room for between ten and thirty minutes to meet their tutor for a form period.

In any school, if you talk to the majority of aspirational pupils they will often say that this moment in the school day is the time they like the least and in their eyes, it is a waste of time! Those pupils who are less motivated will often see a form period as a time when they can misbehave and have some 'sport' with their form tutor.

Pupils who say this are as likely to attend an 'Outstanding' school as one that is in 'measures.' It is so important that school leaders ensure that the pupils' first formal moments in the school day supports the learning that will take place and focuses the pupils on the day ahead.

What can you do?

Provide CPD for teachers on what makes an effective form tutor. Just think for a moment, has this ever been provided in your school? When you look around the staffroom there will be colleagues who are excellent form tutors. They are just the people to deliver this session. By running this CPD you are highlighting to all colleagues that this period of time is as important as all the lessons they deliver.

Ensure there are high quality resources for form tutors. If you really want form time to be used well, provide all the materials that are needed so there is no excuse for poor delivery.

Provide checklists on what should happen each day or on various days of the week so that all staff understand the expectation.

Think carefully about the message sent to other teacher by not giving staff a form group. Sometimes the most effective teachers are not given a form group and this can give the impression to staff that this session is not important.

Finally, ensure that senior leaders are visible during the form period. There should be the same amount of quality assurance of form time as of any other lesson.

'Show staff how important form time really is'

Action 62:

Implement an exit process for pupils who are not following expectations

There will always be some pupils who for a particular reason are reluctant to follow the teacher's expectation in a lesson on a particular day. The teacher will work through their toolbox of behavioural strategies and they will not be making any difference as they struggle to keep the pupil in the classroom.

Other children begin to notice that no sanction is working with this child. Some children will become distracted; begin to follow their lead making it ever harder for the teacher. Those pupils who are motivated to learn will become frustrated that their learning is being disrupted and if it becomes continual they will also think that there is little point in trying to learn in this class.

What can you do?

There are points in every teacher's career when they need to be able to remove a child from a lesson so that they can focus on the learning of the pupils in the classroom and hence many schools have an exit procedure, which a teacher can use to remove a pupil from the lesson.

Most exit procedures have a staged approach so that the child has a number of opportunities to change their behaviour before they are exited from the classroom. At each of these points there may also be a sanction.

When a child reaches the exit point there needs to be a system which manages this process. In some schools the child may be asked to leave the classroom and make their way to a location which is staffed. In other schools the teacher may radio or phone for assistance so that a member of staff comes and collects the child and takes them to another location. There may be an opportunity within the school's MIS (Management information system) that automatically calls a member of staff to the classroom. Whatever the system you use, it must be calm and immediate so that both the teacher and child can move on.

Schools will then have their own system for how long the child remains out of lessons, what sanction is attached to being exited from the classroom and what opportunity there is for reconciliation.

'Children must be able to learn without constant disruptions'

Action 63:

Analyse where the most behaviour infractions are occurring

If you are trying to improve behaviour, particularly in a large school, you have to know the locations and times where the problems occur.

There are two sides to this question. The first is those moments in lesson times when the most issues take place. Secondly the locations where there are issues, whether before school, during break and lunch, or at the end of the school.

In every school there is lots of anecdotal information about this. In the staff room or when groups of colleagues gather there will be comments about certain areas being terrible or certain times. The site team and midday supervisors will also have their view.

It is important that leaders carefully analyse this information so that the views of those with the loudest voices are not taken as the truth whereas the issues may be somewhere else.

What can you do?

If you have an exit procedure from lessons a starting point is to analyse the lessons in the week when the highest number take place and then for each lesson, study the locations in the school where the exits occur.

If your school has a behaviour recording system which also includes the warnings prior to exit, these can also be analysed at the step prior to exit. There will be some teachers and pupils who reach this point and then stop. To one extent the system may have worked as the behaviour may have stopped but the lesson has still been disrupted.

Once this information has been gathered those staff who are on patrol can focus on these 'hot spots' and additional leaders can also be deployed to support these times.

Out of lesson time, the data may not be as scientific but you can ask the site team where and when damage occurs. You can also use pupil focus groups to try and find out the areas where pupils feel least safe. The views of staff can be sought.

Once this information is gathered again it is about increasing staffing at these occasions so that pupils feel safer and those pupils who may cause issues know they are more likely to be seen.

'Deploy your staff where they will have the most impact'

Action 64:

Clear systems for managing break and lunchtime

As teachers we all know that if the break and lunchtimes are a disaster it makes managing behaviour in lessons even harder.

It is also easier to manage behaviour during lesson time. Pupils are always in manageable groups with each group being assigned to at least one adult to look after them. Pupils have clear tasks, which occupy them.

Finally, as leaders we will consider which pupils to put in each class and then teachers will carefully plan where those children sit.

These factors do not apply out of lessons so we need to have clear systems for managing break and lunchtime behaviour.

What can you do?

Firstly, ensure that for each break and lunchtime, teachers are clear on which leaders are supporting them at that time and that those leaders are visible to both pupils and staff.

Ensure that there is a clear rota for which members of staff are on duty for each day. Consider what actions you wish staff to take for each duty point. Some staff will be monitoring children queuing to buy foods, other staff will be looking after playgrounds or multi-use games areas and other staff will be managing the inside of the building.

Leaders need to ensure that all staff are in place at the correct time. If colleagues routinely arrive late for their duty, pupils may have already set their behaviour and it makes it harder for the staff member to reinforce the school expectations.

Ensure that there is a clear system for recording behaviour misdemeanours during these times and that there is also a system for dealing with behaviours. For instance, there may be a cool-off location which pupils can be referred to so incidents do not escalate.

Finally ensure that behaviour is analysed as for action 63 so that changes can be made to improve behaviour.

'Manage break times as carefully as lessons for maximum impact'

Action 65:

What is your alternative to exclusion process to provide breathing space between detentions and exclusions?

Most schools will have a system of detentions, which they will use when children are regularly breaking school rules. If such detentions do not seem to be working or the school feels the misdemeanour is more serious then fixed term exclusions can be used.

However, many schools are concerned about excluding children, as they will be missing education and for many children they can be at risk from a range of safeguarding issues if they are absent from school. Hence many schools will use some type of internal exclusion when the child is removed from lessons and does not have normal break and lunchtime but is still in the care of the schools.

One of the big issues in educational social media in recent years has been the campaign, 'ban the booths'. This was highlighting the use of isolation suites in schools where children would be placed in booths for a school day or multiple days and would not be allowed to communicate with other children.

There is no requirement for schools to legally report how long or how often children are placed in such units as opposed to when a child is given a fixed term exclusion and this must be reported in the school register.

What can you do?

Firstly, consider how often pupils are likely to be placed in internal exclusion and how they can be managed. If it is infrequent and there are small numbers can pupils be supervised by senior members of staff when they are not teaching? Equally could non-teaching staff supervise them when they are not in the classroom?

If numbers are higher or used more frequently, develop a base in an area of the school where pupils can be housed. This can range from a nurture style suite to a very formal isolation space with a booth type system. Some colleagues have very strong views on the latter so carefully consider what you feel is right and engage with governors to explain how the provision will be used.

Finally consider how the unit will be staffed. Can this be achieved by staff having reduced non-contact time, by using gaps on timetables or does a colleague need to be employed to provide the supervision?

'Carefully consider the alternative exclusion provision for your school'

Action 66:

Ensure teachers take responsibility for managing behaviour in lessons

It can be easy for staff in a school to say that managing behaviour is the responsibility of leaders. Then when colleagues feel that the standards of behaviour are declining, they can believe it is the fault of the school leaders.

School leaders can also feel this responsibility and believe it is their fault if behaviour is not as good as they feel it should be. A result can be that leaders take it upon themselves to manage all behaviour infractions from removing children from classrooms to leading detentions.

It could be argued that leaders are responsible for designing the systems to manage behaviour in the school. If there is a decline in standards of behaviour then these systems may need to be looked at and amended.

Managing behaviour though is the responsibility of all staff. If leaders take on this burden alone, and colleagues lose this responsibility they can become disempowered.

What can you do?

If there is an issue in a classroom, establish systems which give the responsibility in the first instance to teachers. If the school has a system where after a certain number of warnings a detention is given. The teacher, possibly as part of their subject team or phase team, should manage this detention.

If pupils are removed from the classroom and moved to a cool-off space, can all teachers be given a role in managing this provision? Or could it be part of a middle leader's role so it is not just seen as a senior management responsibility?

For routine infractions can teachers be given responsibility (with support) of contacting parents to explain the issue and what has happened? If it is felt that a meeting with parents is required, can the teacher lead this meeting with support from a more experienced leader?

'All colleagues have responsibility for managing pupil behaviour'

Action 67:

Conduct a pupil focus group to understand the pupil view of behaviour

In nearly all schools there can be a temptation for teachers to say that behaviour is continually getting worse. Leaders may be aware of these comments and take a different view, that behaviour is acceptable or good, and where it is not, this is the result of indifferent teaching.

Leaders may also perceive that they are aware of the classrooms where behaviour is unacceptable because of their data analysis or their views from walking the school.

Outside of the lesson, leaders may believe that they know the locations where behaviour is poor due to the litter that is left, the vandalism that is caused or the groups of children they see congregating.

However, any of these assumptions can be incorrect and some of the most useful and insightful information can come from the pupils. One way of obtaining their views quickly is to conduct focus groups of different groups of pupils.

What can you do?

Identify a sample of pupils from a particular year group or phase of the school. You are looking for pupils who are unafraid of giving their views.

Design a set of questions to probe issues that you are concerned about. These could include:
1) In which lessons do pupils behave well?
2) In which lessons do you finding learning difficult because of the behaviour of the class?

3) Does the behaviour system [insert its name here] stop pupils behaving badly?
4) At what point in the system do pupils begin to behave?
5) Is there anywhere in school where you feel scared or other pupils feel scared?
6) Are there any times in the school day when you feel scared or other pupils feel scared?
7) What do you think the school could do to improve pupil behaviour?

Think carefully about which member of staff asks the pupils the question. You might ask a non-teacher who children trust to take on this role.

Then triangulate the findings from the focus groups with leaders' understanding of the issues and with behaviour management data, which is collected.

'Ask the pupils where and when they feel scared?'

Action 68:

Tidy up! Smarten up! Check the learning environment supports good behaviour

We have all been into some teachers' classrooms; books and resources are cascading off desks onto the floor, and seemingly every surface in the classroom is covered with a mixture of resources, paper and activities.

We can walk through corridors and find lots of furniture, making walkways feel very narrow and again surfaces covered with all kinds of materials. The noticeboards in corridors may seem uncared for with dated or tattered displays.

In the worst scenario vandalism may be left untreated and litter is left collecting in various locations.

There is no doubt that pupils, and in fact all humans, generally behave worse when the environment does not appear to be cared for. In addition, it has been found that people feel less safe when the environment is left damaged.

What can you do?

Promote a tidy school ethos. At the start or end of the year, have a 'skip' day when teachers are encouraged to empty their classrooms and cupboards. Try and make sure those sets of text books from the 1980s are no longer found hidden in cupboards.

Encourage staff to take a 'less is more' approach to resources left on surfaces. Why not have a Friday clean desk policy when all teacher desks are left clear of materials?

Have regular competitions for the tidiest classroom, classroom with the best displays or classroom with the most creative environment. Involve the children in judging which is the winner.

Conduct regular environment walks possibly with a caretaker or a member of the site team, ensure that actions are recorded and then completed for the next time. Ask a governor or someone who walks the school less often to be harsh and highlight the things that you may be blind to.

If there is any vandalism, make it a priority to be repaired as fast as possible. Some schools will have an aim that any vandalism is repaired immediately to try and stop other pupils seeing it. Finally highlight the issue of litter and develop a school strategy to work together to keep the school and grounds tidy.

'Pupil behaviour is worse when schools look for uncared for'

6 ENSURING HIGH ATTENDANCE

It is a truism that pupils will not learn and will not make progress if they are not in school. For many schools increasing pupil attendance can be a difficult challenge. There are times when it is felt that attendance has stalled and there is nothing that we can do to improve the situation.

Equally we can also feel that of all measures the one that we can improve fastest is pupil attendance. It does not matter if the previous teaching has been poor, this does not affect attendance. Instead on the first day of every year, every child has 100%.

Those schools with high attendance, particularly those in challenging areas, recognise that creating high attendance and then maintaining it requires relentless efforts. It does not happen by accident but instead schools develop systems and actions which have an impact.

They will constantly re-engineer them to ensure that they stay fresh and continue to be effective.

As with the previous three chapters, this one provides a range of actions which you can take to try and drive up the attendance of pupils in your school. Some will have an immediate impact; others will require time and effort to give longer-term benefit.

The following table allows you to track which actions you have implemented over the course of the academic year and the Key Stage they are most applicable too. For that day in day out improvement, keep returning to them and decide if further actions should be implemented or if those already implemented are having an impact. Annotate the table to show which are in place for each term.

At the end of year, you should ask yourself two questions:

- What has been the impact?
- What do we need to do differently to maintain / increase the impact?

Figure 6.1: Summary of actions to improve attendance

	Action	Primary	Secondary	T1	T2	T3
69	Study the attendance data for the previous academic year	*	*			
70	Develop an attendance sprint	*	*			
71	Track attendance of individual pupils on a daily basis	*	*			
72	Calculate attendance statistics weekly, every week	*	*			
73	Begin with the attendance of the previous year	*	*			
74	Gather attendance transition information	*	*			
75	Which strategies work with which children?	*	*			
76	Share attendance data with	*	*			

	staff					
77	Follow up absence with phone calls	*	*			
78	Develop a graded set of absence letters	*	*			
79	Know and understand your context	*	*			
80	Have school rewards for high attendance	*	*			
81	Build family support for high attendance	*	*			
82	Getting to Green	*	*			
83	Power attendance with displays	*	*			
84	Pick Up Children	*	*			
85	Target Persistent Absence	*	*			
86	Model positive conversations	*	*			
87	Focus on the attendance of disadvantaged pupils	*	*			
88	Develop attendance support plans	*	*			
89	Have a system for dealing with 'lates'	*	*			

ENSURING HIGH ATTENDANCE

THE ACTIONS

Action 69:

Study the attendance data for the previous academic year

The starting point for building the attendance in any school is to look at the historical information. When you look at a new school, there is obviously information on the school performance table, which will show overall attendance and rates of persistent absence information for the school.

This will show you the highlights or lowlights of attendance but the pastoral information publicly available is usually a year behind the academic information. You do not know if attendance has rapidly improved, remained consistent or even fallen off a proverbial cliff.

What can you do?

As soon as national data is available, you need to be aware of the headline measures so that you know where the school is in comparison to national measures. What was overall attendance for the school and what was persistent absence? If you are joining a school mid-year what are those figures for the year so far?

What are the broad trends in performance over the last three years in terms of overall attendance and persistent absence? Is there a consistent trend or is it 'bumpy'? What does this tell you about what you may expect this year if systems remain the same?

Then start to look at the detail by finding answers to the following questions:
- Which days had poor attendance? Why?
- Which weeks had poor attendance? Why?
- Which groups of pupils? Why?
- Which families?

Once you have this information, you can begin to consider what actions or systems you may need to introduce to improve or maintain attendance at the school.

'Pupils attendance is often systemic; the past can show you the future'

Action 70:

Develop an attendance sprint

The idea of sprints has already been suggested in previous sections. In summary, it is found in all organisations that if all colleagues focus on an element of improvement at the same time, this is far more powerful than different individuals working on it in a fragmented fashion.

We also find in schools that if all colleagues work on one element at the same time, children will accept the change far quicker and will not play colleagues off against each other.

In any sprint, you need to carefully plan what actions you are all going to take. It is often more effective if the actions build up over time rather than trying to complete every single action on the first day of the sprint.

What can you do?

Ensure that all staff members focus on attendance as a high priority for the first month of the term, so that pupils do not get into bad habits. If we can get attendance right at the start of the term, it will stay right for longer.

Work with your staff before the start of term, preferably at the end of the previous term to consider what actions all can take that will improve attendance or maintain it.

The focus here is what everyone can do together so that there is a total consistency amongst all colleagues and pupils know what to expect from everybody.

In this discussion we need to highlight that attendance is everyone's issue not something that is abdicated to an attendance officer or a certain member of the SLT.

Write down the daily actions, which all teachers will take with the dates on when they will occur and ensure that leaders keep checking that they are being carried out. Do not assume they are happening. As soon as you assume they are, they are probably not taking place.

'We can improve attendance quicker if we all work together'

Action 71:

Track attendance of individual pupils on a daily basis

School attendance is about individual pupils. Yes, we calculate statistics on what the attendance for a school is on a daily basis and calculate averages on a weekly, termly or yearly basis. However, it all comes down to individual pupils being in school day after day, every day.

There is a danger that senior leaders can forget about the individuals in their drive for improvement and their eagerness to see statistics begin to move in the right direction.

Equally, it is no good to only receive attendance information on individual pupils for the morning session after lunch or even the next day.

There are schools where pupils appear in drift into school at varying points in the morning and the single colleague with responsibility for attendance figures is overwhelmed. Leaders receive information late and it is often inaccurate. In such a situation, attendance will not improve

What can you do?

The attendance of all individuals must be carefully and accurately gathered. It also must be completed as speedily as possible.

You need to know which children are in school and every day, be constantly looking at how their individual attendance is changing. You need to be asking yourself questions such as these:
- Which pupils have had three days off in a row?
- Which pupils are averaging one day off a week?
- Which children are always off a Monday?
- Which children are slipping into persistent absence?

This can only be determined if you have accurate tracking of individual children on a daily basis.

'Improving attendance starts with individual pupils'

Action 72:

Calculate attendance statistics weekly, every week

When we look at schools where the attendance has deteriorated over time it is often found that leaders were unclear on where the issues were. There are many schools that do not routinely calculate the persistent absence figures: in fact, there are some Headteachers and school leaders who are unclear as to what persistent absence actually is. At best they may be calculating the overall attendance figure and that is all.

Attendance is one of the most straightforward pieces of school data to track as it is binary; pupils are in school or absent and the data should be available every day, twice a day.

In addition, even the most minimal school management information systems will immediately complete calculations to produce the statistics required.

Yet too often, there are schools where senior leaders do not look at attendance data as a matter of course and as a result attendance of pupils will drift.

What can you do?

You must ensure that for every session, mornings and afternoon, the overall attendance is calculated and shared with senior leaders.

One leader must have responsibility for ensuring that this is completed every day and that the attendance is continually compared with what happened on previous days. This must always happen.

Then on a weekly basis, the trends must be considered:

- Which year groups have the lowest attendance?
- Which day of the week is attendance the lowest?
- How does the attendance of PP children compare with non-PP children?
- How does the attendance for different prior attainment groups compare?
- What is the attendance for key marginal children?

This information is vital in enabling leaders to begin to take interventions to improve attendance and also to consider if interventions are making a difference.

Indeed, sometimes we find that the act of leaders carefully analysing attendance and being aware of the detail of what is happening in schools can provide some improvement on its own.

'If you don't know where you are, how do you work out where to go?'

Action 73:

Begin with the attendance from the previous year

In many schools at the beginning of the academic year, senior leaders can feel that they are spending the first few days watching what is occurring around the school.

If there are training days these can feel hectic as everyone is trying to get the school ready for the new academic year. Day one with the children can often be time for assemblies and familiarisation and then when normal lessons begin, if senior leaders have a reduced timetable they may have a pause in proceedings.

It is against this backdrop that attendance may not immediately be at the top of anyone's priority list. Instead the refrain can be, 'let's leave it a couple of weeks and see how the pupils' attendance settles down and after all it's just random if a pupil has a number of absences in those first few days!'

There is some sense in this logic in that calculating persistent absence in the first few weeks can be misleading as a child missing one day in the first two weeks, statistically is labelled as P.A.

What can you do?

The schools with the most effective attendance strategies will take a different view as they recognise that ground can be quickly lost in the battle to achieve high attendance and bad habits rapidly become normal practice. Attendance specialists tell us that poor attendance will be something that has been consistent over a number of years.

To avoid this schools will begin the year by looking at historic attendance. There are two ways of looking at this. You can take the attendance from the whole of last year and target those children who were PA at the end of the year and as soon as they have any absence you begin to use your attendance systems to try and catch them before they become PA for this year too.

The other tactic to take is look at last year's attendance just for this one-month period. You can find that there are some children who always have poor attendance at the start of the year. Their attendance will improve over the year but the learning remains lost. This often occurs in locations where seasonal working is the norm or when the weather is nice pupils will decide to enjoy the weather rather than the classroom. So those pupils who had poor attendance last September, as soon as they are absent again begin to use your attendance systems.

In addition, some schools will be pre-emptive by looking at children who fall into either of these groups and communicate with the children or their families before the start of term to encourage good attendance from the first day.

'Use last year's attendance as a starting point'

Action 74:

Gather attendance transition information

In both secondary schools and those primary schools that only admit KS2 pupils we take it as read that we need to gather the attainment data from the previous Key Stage. Admittedly in the world of CTF transfers the information will be moved straight into our MIS system.

Experienced EYFS practitioners will often try and find time in the summer term to visit children either in their pre-school setting or sometimes even undertake home visits all with the aim of trying to establish the needs of the children before they begin the academic year.

Yet attendance is often the Cinderella factor in our collection of information from previous settings. This is peculiar as we recognise that low attendance is a habit that builds up over time and any information that we have will support our attendance management processes.

What can you do?

As part of the transition process, gather information from feeder schools and settings on historic attendance of the pupils. Ask the school if they would share the child's overall attendance over each of the last three years and if attendance is low for any of those years, could they explain why?

If pupils have had low attendance and it has then improved, could the school explain the strategies that they used and proved effective? This could have been meetings with parents which were positive or perhaps it was the final attendance letter with notification that the next action would be a fixed penalty notice which provided the necessary impetus.

They may also share information about the family's view of school attendance and how positively or not they engaged with any school processes. Admittedly parents may engage differently with different settings but it is always useful to have prior information.

They could also be asked about any other siblings. Do they have similar patterns of attendance? Or are they markedly different and if so what can they explain why this has happened?

When you have this information, you can then begin to work with children and families straight away rather than wait to see if there is a pattern in attendance.

'Which strategies were effective in the previous school?'

Action 75:

Which strategies work with which children?

When we are teaching our classes, we are aware of which intervention strategies have the most impact upon which children. There are some children who require a second explanation, some children where pre-teaching makes the difference and other children who respond positively to interventions outside of the school day.

The same is true when we are trying to improve behaviour of children, we know which tactics will improve a child's behaviour and which will have the opposite effect. At a very basic level we know which child will heed warnings and which children will alter their behaviour as a result of a sanction. We also know which children will actually behave worse as a result of different interventions.

The same intelligence needs to be gathered as to which attendance strategies will have the biggest impact to improve attendance for individual children.

What can you do?

When an attendance intervention is applied with an individual child, consider the impact that is has. Try not to use multiple attendance strategies at the same time so you can identify which has made the difference.

Think of the basic interventions such as:
- Attendance rewards
- Phone call to parents
- Letters to parents
- Visiting the house
- Attendance meetings
- Threats of fine

Then group the action into one of the four categories:

- Positive response from family and improved the child's attendance
- Negative response from parents but still improved child's attendance
- Positive response from family but no impact on child's attendance
- Negative response from family and impact on child's attendance

Use this information to help personalise the actions that you take to improve attendance of individual children.

'Different actions have different impacts for different children and families'

Action 76:

Share attendance data with staff

As with so many school improvement priorities, they are most effective when the whole school staff are focussed on making the difference.

If the school staff are to be committed to making the issue better firstly they need to know why it is important. This must be rooted in the impact it has on the young people and not on an OFSTED rating.

There are lots of attendance statistics available which show the impact of certain percentage points and the number of days missed over a child's school career, the difference it makes to children's attainment and even the links between attendance and a range of social issues.

Secondly, they need to be aware of what the school is trying to achieve. Is there a certain attendance target that you are aiming for?

Thirdly, leaders need to share the current position and how this is changing over time.

What can you do?

Firstly, communicate the attendance 'why' clearly and succinctly and ensure this message is repeated.

Secondly share the targets that you are working towards in a format that people understand.

Thirdly leaders should regularly share attendance data with all staff. Tutors and classroom teachers should be told the attendance of the children they look after on a weekly basis and how it is changing. They should also be aware of the attendance of their class. In a small primary school, the attendance of all the classes would be shared so that teachers can see how different classes compare. In a secondary school, teachers would have the attendances of the other classes in their year group or phase. They would also be told of the overall school attendance and the impact their class or year has on the overall totals.

Finally, leaders who are responsible for certain key groups of children should communicate with staff the particular challenges a group of children are facing. E.g. the pupil premium lead will communicate the gap between the attendance of PP children and that for all children, and the SENCO will share similar information about the attendance of SEND children. When key groups are small and individual pupils can be identified this information should not be shared at a whole school level.

'Attendance is everyone's priority'

Action 77:

Follow up absences with phone calls

It is now common practice in most schools that phone calls will be made to parents when children are absent from school. It is not too long ago that this would have been considered unusual but now we all recognise it is important.

Safeguarding reasons are probably key to this becoming the norm in most schools. The first reason was to establish if children had gone missing on their way to school so that safeguarding processes could be put into place if this was the case. It is the worst nightmare for parents and teachers, that a child sets off to school and never gets there.

This has now evolved into custom and practice to try and support attendance of children in schools and discourage parents from keeping children off school when they should be present.

What can you do?

First day call is vital and should be made each day, every day. The sooner that these calls can be completed the better. In some schools, a member of the support staff may be given the title of Attendance Officer and be responsible for making all the calls. However, this can mean that it can take a while for all the calls to be completed. There can also be a clash of priorities in making all the calls and completing the attendance statistics. In larger schools it may be more effective to deploy a number of staff for the first hour of the day so that all calls can be completed in as timely a fashion as possible.

Staff can sometimes slow the process down as there will be an occasion when they have called a parent and the child was in school and not absent. Unfortunately, mistakes do happen but this should not be a reason for the calls to slow down.

Some schools will provide a script for their support staff of what they should say when they make the calls. The script will change as the length of the absence increases. Leaders need to think carefully as to the message they wish their staff to deliver and also how it can be worded to reduced confrontation. The script may be tweaked for a specific circumstance but only with the agreement of a more senior member of staff.

'First day call is a non-negotiable'

Action 78:

Develop a graded set of absence letters

There are many leaders who believe that developing effective systems are key to driving improvement. We wish to avoid actions being missed or being amended and hence the consistency of the system failing.

At the same time, if we have well thought out and effective systems in place this should save time for all colleagues as they just move to the next step in the sequence for dealing with the issue.

In addition, systems can stop people feeling that they are being treated unfairly as the same action will be taken at the same point with all people. In the same way that you can develop a set of scripts for attendance phone calls, it is good practice to develop a set of letters, which are sent out at different points in dealing with pupil attendance.

What can you do?

The first stage is to look at the letter at the start of the process and towards the end of the process. The first letter will be sent out when a child's attendance is below a certain trigger point. This could be a certain number of absences in a single term or it could be linked to a statistic such as persistent absence. The letter will re-iterate the importance of high attendance and the impact that non-attendance has on learning.

At the end of the process will be the letter which notifies the parents that due to attendance being so low, a fixed penalty notice will be issued. Leaders then need to fill in the gaps in between these two letters and decide at which point letters will be sent out and what will the consequence be.

Many schools will have attendance management meetings where they invite the parent and child into school to discuss how attendance can be improved and what support they require. There can be more punitive meetings as the process moves closer to a penalty notice which could involve governors.

The important thing is that the sequence is organised with appropriate triggers and then leaders can ask for a breakdown of the number of pupils at each stage of the process.

'Consistent systems drive improvement'

Action 79:

Know and understand your context

Prior to the growth of the academy movement, term times were generally very straight forwards as all schools in the local authority would have the same term times with maybe some slight alterations as to when a school placed their training/inset days or chose to disaggregate them when they wished.

If children lived close to a county boundary they might find their terms would be different from a school only a couple of miles away. This may mean that siblings in a primary school in one county may have different term dates to a sibling in a secondary school in a different county.

Term times are now far more fragmented with academies having the power to set their own holidays. This often means that the placement of training/inset days is very different. Some schools are trialling two-week half terms particularly in October which has a knock-on somewhere else in the term. In addition, some MATs may have organised the same term dates over their whole network to support school improvement but this can have a knock on to attendance in a certain locality.

What can you do?

The first step is to liaise with schools in your community and see if you can agree training days as much as you can. If one school has a term day when another has a teacher training day, this can easily affect school attendance. This is more important at the start of the academic year when we want children to form good attendance habits.

If your school has slightly different dates to your feeder school, you can remind parents of this in your letters so that a common message is sent out. For example, 'we have a training day but a reminder that 'x' schools are in term, so please make sure that any siblings still attend their school'.

Some groups of schools have been more creative and looked at the context in their local community and planned holidays accordingly. One example is a coastal holiday town where parents generally cannot take time off in the summer and if they did holidays are very expensive. Instead they have placed a two week break during the autumn term so that parents can have family holidays at a reduced price.

'Work with local schools to improve attendance'

Action 80:

Have school rewards for high attendance

High attendance does not just happen as the previous set of actions in this chapter have shown. Primary and secondary schools who have really improved have found a mechanism to ensure that all children want the attendance to be high in the school. The children want to make sure they are at school as often as possible, they also want to encourage their class mates to be in school as often as possible.

The key is in that paragraph, the children want to be in school. This cannot be achieved by sanctions, there needs to be a desire for children to want to be in school.

What can you do?

The first and most important thing is that lessons need to be interesting. If teachers provide lessons that pupils find stimulating they will wish to be in school.

You can see some great examples on social media where teachers have made exciting scenes to inspire reading: from crime scenes, to dinosaurs walking through classrooms, to magic beans bursting into life. Schools need to create an environment in which pupils want to find out what happens next.

Pupils also generally like competition. Most schools will have house competitions for different events. Running attendance competitions is really important and giving pupils feedback on the class attendance and their impact towards this is important. This communication can be a simple as signs on classroom doors to those schools and Trusts who use social media to communicate their best attendance.

Giving some kind of reward at a regular basis is also important. Whilst many schools have trophies or shields for end of term attendance this can be a long way off. So, presenting the award on a weekly basis keeps the pupils' focus.

Whilst it does not fit in with healthy schools, many schools will award a tub of chocolates for the class with the best attendance or the most improved attendance.

Senior leaders can make a big event out of this weekly prize and again it all gives a positive focus on school attendance, which pupils and teachers can use as a source of motivation.

'Give attendance a positive spin'

Action 81:

Build family support for high attendance

A second lever to improving attendance is to gain the support of parents and families to provide a greater incentive for children to be in school. For many children it is the parents who are the real gatekeeper to increase attendance.

They make the decision as to whether the child should be in school or not. They will encourage and cajole children to get up in a morning and set the culture of high attendance for children.

Schools need to work with families to encourage their support as well as using the sanctions and warnings discussed earlier in this chapter.

What can you do?

Communicate clearly and succinctly the impact low and high attendance has on children. There are some excellent cartoons on social media which show the impact of missing a day here and day there and hence over a child's school career how many days they are missing.

There are other statistics which you can find which show the effect low and high attendance has on children's grades which you can also share with parents.

However, it is also important to turn attendance into positivity. There are many schools who use their social media, Twitter or Facebook accounts to really share their attendance good news. This takes a concerted effort by school staff to engage in this celebration. One tweet or one post will not make much difference.

In some MATs you will see the competition between local schools over which has the highest or most improved attendance which can engage the local community and gain their support.

Finally, schools in very deprived areas have thought long and hard about the rewards they can offer families whose children have strong attendance.

There are some schools who on weekly basis will have a raffle for all children who have had 100% attendance for the week and the prize will be a family meal whether that is a meal deal from a local supermarket or a family meal from a takeaway. Again, it may not be healthy meals but it can provide an encouragement to give attendance a boost.

Schools who have used this approach have even used their pupil premium funding for the year to fund the prizes. Other schools have been fortunate enough to gain sponsorship from local shops.

'It is families who get the children into school'

Action 82:

Get to Green

Many children and even families can become disenfranchised by the attempts of schools to improve attendance as they often focus on the 100% attendance of children being in each day and every day.

This is of course the holy grail of pupil attendance but for some pupils and families the focus on this means they feel they can never succeed. It can feel to them a little like a teacher only giving feedback on whether children are achieving 'Greater Depth' or a 'Grade 9' when children are struggling to reach 'pre-Key Stage' or a 'Grade 1'.

Schools need to focus on how they can encourage children to improve their attendance and give them feedback. Schools create many systems to do this process and 'Get to Green' is one that is seen used.

What can you do?

Each form or class group gets a list of the average attendance for the last two weeks. The aim is that for this week, children have to try and get an attendance higher than the fortnight average and if they do the square is colour coded. Over the course of the term, they can see how many green squares they can collect.

For the first two weeks of the new academic year, their average attendance from the previous year is used.

Figure 6.2: Getting to Green

Name	Average	Week1	Green?	Average	Week2	Green?	Average	Week3	Green?
	95%	90%		95%	90%		90%	100%	G
	96%	100%	G	96%	90%		95%	100%	G
	98%	100%	G	98%	100%	G	100%	100%	G

It is important to explain to the children what the attendance figures means and what they have to do in practice to 'get to green'.

For example, 'Child A' had an historical attendance from the previous year of 95%. The child needs it explained that if they miss a half day over the week, their attendance would be 90%. So, to beat 95%, they have to be in school for the full week.

In the first two week's 'Child A' missed a morning each week so by week 3 their fortnightly average is 90%. They have a full week of attendance in week 3, so have got to green!

'Praise children for improving their attendance'

Action 83:

Power Attendance using school displays

One of the most visible displays of how a school is supporting the children is the use its make of displays. The environment the children work in is vital in sharing message with the children.

This has already been written about in action 52 about working walls and also action 67, which looked at how the learning environment can support good behaviour.

Displays have to be high quality to show the children the issue is important. There are countless stories where new Headteachers have begun the turnaround of a new school and the first thing they have done is had the school repainted to send a message to the children of positivity and care.

Unfortunately, there are still schools where displays of attendance are not of a high quality. Instead there is untidy board for form notices where you will find the information related to attendance. There will be scruffy signs on the classroom door and attendance figures may be handwritten on a white board which has become smeared with use.

This does not send a message that the school is really concerned about pupil attendance.

What can you do?

In the entrance areas for children ensure there are high quality displays which explain to children why it is important they come to school. Make sure these are changed regularly.

In areas where parents come into the school, have a set of displays which explains pupil attendance from a parent perspective including support parents can access.

On every classroom door, in the school house style, have a notice which explains that class or tutor groups attendance for the year compared to the target.

Change the design of the poster each half term to engage with pupils. If the class has received a reward or prize for attendance these could be collected about the door so that they build up over the year.

Inside the classroom have an age appropriate display about the importance of attendance. This should include the daily attendance figure or the attendance for the week so far depending on the school's process. This display should look as good as any other display in the classroom.

'Care taken over displays gives a powerful message'

Action 84:

Pick Up Children

The attitude towards attendance in schools has very much changed. The view now is every day really does count and every day missed is a vital day of learning lost. This means that schools are considering actions that they would never have taken in the past.

It would have been an anathema in the past for teachers or support staff to go and do home visits to encourage attendance but with the right risk assessments it can be an important tool available to schools.

In rural areas children only have one opportunity to get to school and that is the school bus. If they miss that bus, even by a minute, there are often no public services so the child loses the whole day of education for the sake of being one minute late up in the morning or perhaps nipping back into the house to collect something that they have forgotten in a rush to get out. Primary age children may also catch buses and it is difficult for parents to sometimes get the child to the bus stop on time.

What can you do?

Most secondary schools have a minibus available to them, which is often sitting in the school grounds doing nothing. Can the use of this be planned into the attendance team's daily duties?

In rural areas, a simple mistake easily costs a day's learning an innocent error in year 7 can lead to a habit of low attendance later on in the school.

Once the registers have been completed, target those children in rural locations especially disadvantaged children to see if they have missed the bus and if so organise a route so that the children can be collected and brought to school.

Some schools in urban areas have trialled the same type of system to knock on doors of the house and try and encourage children into school. Some schools will use a system of telephoning those pupils who live further afield with the offer of collecting them so that they are only a little bit late.

A different approach that some schools take is to home visit children with low attendance to see what the issue is with that day and whether the excuse is not a real reason but a made-up one. This type of approach needs careful risk assessment as you can be dealing with more challenging parents.

'Every single day's learning really does count'

Action 85:

Target Persistent Absence

If attendance is particularly low or high, it can sometimes feel that all the actions being taken do not drastically change the overall attendance figures. Indeed, moving the attendance figure can sometimes feel a little like changing the direction of an oil tanker. At the beginning, the change of direction is barely visible and seems very slow.

Persistent Absence is an area where you can see movement in the statistics more quickly, especially if a forensic approach to persistent absence is adopted. As we know, persistent absence is those children who have an attendance of less than 90%. In effect they miss one day of schooling every fortnight or two days a month. These are often the children who just have the odd day off often with no pattern but these days here and there mount up and they become persistently absent pupils.

From a learning point of view, these pupils will often miss assessments or key lessons and have haphazard gaps in their learning. This discontinuity can be far more damaging than the child who misses a whole week for illness.

What can you do?

As in previous actions, the first task is analysis to make sure you have accurate lists of those children who are persistently absent (PA). Look at the children and see if there are patterns in their absence. Do they regularly miss a Monday or Friday? Do they seem to miss certain lessons? If you can see such patterns, the pastoral team needs to talk to the child and see what support can be given. Dealing with absence often needs to move from punitive to support.

Next look at the children who are only just PA: the children who have attendance between 85% and 90%. These are your quick wins. Calculate how many days of continuous attendance will they need so they move out of the PA category. At different points of the term, the number of days will vary.

Again, using the pastoral team, work with those children individually and explain to them the concept of PA and how this could affect them in the world of work. Set them challenges of how many days of attendance they need to be no longer PA. Then check in on them every day to see if they are in school.

Ensure you praise them if they are in-school every day. You could look at small rewards if you feel this is appropriate. This could be a simple as a written note or card saying that you are proud of them for the effort that they are making.

Once you have move some of these children out of the PA category, then start working with the next group of children and trying to move them. With this kind of forensic approach, schools can quickly make a difference.

'Focus forensically on persistent absence'

Action 86:

Model positive conversations

There are some children who find attendance at school challenging for all kinds of reasons. It can be a lack of family support at home, it can be pastoral challenges that they are facing, it can be difficulties in family finance or it can mental health problems that they are having.

For these reasons it is vital that all school staff consider carefully the conversations that they are having with children in care as saying the wrong thing at the wrong time can have a far bigger impact that we realise. As the quotation says, 'everyone you meet is fighting a battle you know nothing about'.

Staff need to be so careful about the sarcastic comments they make to children. They may say that they are only joking but such comments can set children back. In addition, other children will hear them, pick up on them and then repeat them as they can feel they have permission to use such phrases. Things we need to look out for include:

- 'I'd forgotten what you looked like'
- 'Have you had a good holiday'
- 'You must be well rested now after your break'

What can you do?

Firstly, explain to all staff that there is no place in the school for such sarcastic comments, even if they are meant as jokes or banter. Staff are the adults, they are the professionals and should be doing everything they can to improve attendance.

Be explicit with staff about the type of comments they need to be avoid and point out the negative impact they can have on children.

Work with staff about how they can have positive conversations with children about their attendance. Use verbal praise when you can when children are in school.

Find opportunities for caring conversations with children when they have been off to see if any support is required. Too often we expect children to just jump back into lessons without seeing how we can help them with aspects of learning that they have missed.

In essence it is about continually building a positive and caring culture in your school, which supports all children. This does not happen by accident and leaders cannot just assume that it is happening.

'Caring conversations really make the difference'

Action 87:

Focus on the attendance of disadvantaged pupils

One of the significant gaps in performance of many schools is the outcomes achieved by disadvantaged pupils. At a national level they still lag behind other pupils. This is mirrored in the attendance of disadvantaged pupils. This is often significantly lower than all pupils.

The upside of this is that if you can increase the attendance of disadvantaged pupils in a school then by its nature, the attendance of all pupils will increase.

Another way of thinking about this is that if the disadvantaged pupils have a good day, a good week or even a good month of attendance then the same will have been achieved for the whole school.

In turn because there are a smaller number of disadvantaged pupils in most schools then there are a smaller number of children to focus on.

What can you do?

The first task is always to do the analysis. When you have the attendance figures of pupils drill down into the disadvantaged pupils and then move that lens even closer and focus in on individual pupils.

Place them into five groups.

Figure 6.3: Five categories of pupil attendance

Description	Attendance Figures
Good attendance	Over 95%
At risk of PA	90% to 95%
Borderline PA children	85% to 90%
Poor attendance	80% to 85%
Serious Concerns	Less than 80%

Constantly keep looking at the individual pupils in these groups and whether you have pupils moving in the right directions.

In any school, there are always limited resources so consider whether you should focus on the disadvantaged children first.

If this is seen as the right approach, then these are the pupils who are telephoned first in a morning. If pupils are being collected, make sure these pupils are picked up first. If pupils are receiving supportive conversations, speak to the disadvantaged pupils. There are leaders who believe that a school should always look at the additional extra provided for disadvantaged pupils and one way to do this is to make sure they are your first focus of intervention.

'If disadvantaged pupils have a good day, so does the whole school'

Action 88:

Attendance Support Plans

It is very common in schools to have a whole range of support plans for children. These range from the very formal EHCP for high needs SEN pupils, to support plans for pupils on the SEND register to behaviour support plans. Frequently the same style of support plans are not used to improve attendance.

There is no reason why the same format cannot be used to consider how those pupils with poor attendance or poor punctuality can be best supported by the community to ensure that they are in school as often as possible.

What can you do?

Firstly, look at the support plans in use in the school and ensure if there is a common format and then also use this for attendance reasons.

Consider the actions in this section and all the other interventions that are used in your school to support attendance and this then provides the menu of support that the school can offer to pupils to support their attendance at schools.

Then consider a list of actions that parents could take to support their child's attendance and alongside this as the children become older what they can do for themselves to improve their attendance.

In addition, the school needs to consider how the child can be praised or rewarded for improvements in their attendance. This can involve reminding the child of the structures in the school that all pupils can receive and how the child can get there.

There are some pupils who need rewards breaking down into very little steps especially when they are working from a low basis. E.g. if the reward is based on full attendance for a half term, there will be some children who 'fail' in the first week.

The most important thing about any support plan is the conversation held at the start of the process and the on-going conversations had during the plan. Really trying to unpick what the issues are, what leads to low attendance and then mentoring the child moving forwards could be just the catalyst to really make a change in behaviour.

'Supportive conversations go hand in hand with any support plan'

Action 89:

Have a system for dealing with 'lates'

This action is purposefully placed as the last in the attendance section. Once you have improved your attendance as much as you believe is possible then is the time to squeeze the punctuality to get that as strong as possible too.

Sometimes you see schools trying to improve punctuality almost too soon and as a result the attendance decreases. The classic example of this is the school that has weak attendance and punctuality. There is not a culture of high attendance in the school. The school tries to work on both issues at the same time and decides to take a punitive approach to lateness.

So, if a child arrives late for school and is given a break time detention. As there is not a culture of high attendance in the school, the next time the child is late, they think rather than getting the detention they might as well not come into school until after break, at lunchtime or even not come in at all.

What can you do?

The first stage is to think carefully as to whether there is a culture of high attendance in the school and make this the prime focus of intervention. Once this is in place then squeeze lateness.

Decide where the school is in terms of overall attendance. The use this to determine if there is going to be punitive approach to lateness and if so what is the tolerance. Does the school take a zero-tolerance approach of immediate sanction for any lateness? Or does the school give each child the benefit of the doubt for occasional lateness?

Schools may say they never punish lateness but instead they look to see how they can support pupils in being punctual and always take a positive approach and praise pupils for being on-time.

Ensure that careful statistics are kept on lates. This is easier to do if there is only one way into a school and support staff can then monitor the time of arrival of all pupils. Thinking of action 85, model the conversations that support staff have with late pupils. It can be very easy for these to turn into negative or sarcastic comments which can lead to confrontation.

Carefully analyse the statistics for lateness. Are there trends of punctuality? Are there certain days prone for lateness? Is a particular year group a problem? Then look at building your systems around this.

'Beware of unintended consequences of placing a squeeze on lateness'

7 ENDNOTE

Let us return to the title of the book, 'No silver bullets – Day in, day out school improvement'. This book captures a range of school improvement actions that I have seen utilised in so many different schools. The order in which they are written does not imply the order in which they should be implemented in a school.

Instead as a leader you need to think where are the issues in the school or where you want to focus improvement and then consider which of these actions will make the difference at your school.

School improvement does take time: this does not mean that you should not work at pace as you have to ensure that all children receive the education that they require. Instead what you have to do is to carefully consider how many actions are appropriate to implement in your school at any given time and then how long is required to ensure that they are embedded in the school before moving onto the next one.

There are too many schools who have thrown every action at the school at the same time, school staff have not been able to cope with the number of initiatives and too many have failed. They were not the wrong initiatives they were just implemented poorly.

In addition, beware of the implementation dip, they might be the right action but it just takes a little time before they have required impact you are looking for.

Finally, school improvement is an exciting journey, there will be good days and bad days but if you keep working with your staff, keep fine tuning and keep refocusing, then you will improve your school. You do not need to look for any magic silver bullets. It is a question of the whole staff working towards day in, day out school improvement.

ABOUT THE AUTHOR

Paul K Ainsworth has had Director of School Improvement roles in four Multi Academy Trusts. He has supported leaders of small rural primaries to large 11-18 urban secondary schools, working intensively with those in OFSTED categories or have had a dip in results including three schools that moved from inadequate to good.

He is the author of nine books including 'Get that Teaching Job', 'Middle Leadership' and 'The Senior Leader's Yearbook', a TEDx speaker and a regular presenter at national conferences.

Follow him on twitter at @pkainsworth

'Paul, as a colleague of yours for a number of years and someone who admires and respects your leadership skills and personal touch, let me say what an asset you are to the profession. Everyone I speak to who has worked with you sings your praises - me included.'
Simon Rose
National Executive Director of Primary Education.
David Ross Education Trust.

'You have such a wealth of knowledge and experience. I couldn't have done the turnaround without your support.'
Jonathan Harris
Headteacher.
Sir Herbert Leon Academy.

'I loved working with you during my time at David Ross Education Trust. You have so much experience and valuable skills, that any school or MAT would be fortunate to capitalise upon! Above all, you're one of the nicest and kindest people I've had the pleasure of meeting.'
Suneta Bagri
Former Executive Header
Every Teacher Matters Project.

'Definitely someone I would recommend. Really knows his stuff and his passion for ensuring a great education for all shines through.'
Wendy Baxter
Regional Director.
David Ross Education Trust.

'You have been such a help to me in my leadership journey so far, as well as being a great sounding board for all things CPD related.'
Emma Marshall
Principal.
Havelock Academy.

'I really recommend Paul. He provided invaluable mentoring for me as a new Head in an inadequate school as well as supporting the school to move from inadequate to good in 18 months in his role as Chair of our governing body. He is also one of the nicest people you are ever likely to meet or work with!'
Dominque Osborne,
Executive Headteacher
Edward Heneage Primary Academy.

'I was always so grateful for your expert educational advice for our comms. A valued colleague and advisor for leaders and members of the team across the Trust.'
Emma Wallace
Marketing and Communications Consultant

'I've worked with Paul for many years and I recommend him very highly. He knows school/MAT improvement inside out.'
David Surfleet
Regional Director.
Juniper Education Group.

'Paul worked closely with all head teachers and senior leaders within the academy trust. His support to me and my deputy was invaluable and each visit to the school brought fresh ideas and suggestions on how to improve. We benefitted from his many years of school leadership experience and implementing his suggestions had great impact on the school, staff and children.'
Catherine McHale
Headteacher.

'As a new Headteacher Paul was instrumental in helping me to understand the importance of emotional intelligence and relating to your team at every level with empathy and understanding. He was a fantastic mentor that taught me to look outwards and beyond my own context to drive school improvements and we have since gone from strength to strength.'
Jenna Withers
Headteacher
St Norbert's Primary School.

'A fantastic Chair for the Trust and a role model for other chairs and governors. We will miss you massively.'
Maria Maltby
Head of Governance.
David Ross Education Trust.

'His knowledge of school improvement practice, secured through his own extensive secondary sector experiences including leading the Trust's Teaching School, has made his role of Chair of our Academy Improvement Board extremely effective. Paul's expertise in planning and delivering the NOQSL and NPQML courses has created a new generation of aspiring senior and middle leaders, ably equipped for the challenges of modern school leadership.'

Heather Grundy
Headteacher.

PRAISE FOR 'NO SILVER BULLETS'

'This brilliant book is a 'must have' for any school leader. It is packed full of realistic strategies that can be adopted, adapted and implemented as part of any school improvement journey. Paul carefully captures his own successes, sharing golden threads of advice and quick wins that when applied day in day out will help any school to be great!'
Sarah Paul
Headteacher
Wyberton Primary Academy

'No Silver Bullets is Paul Ainsworth. It is packed to the brim with practical advice for school improvement that is founded in his real-life work. I found Paul's book sage, well balanced and real. Success really is day in day out grind and no glamour, Paul highlights this pragmatic view with a powerhouse of strategies that will make a difference in all schools across the country. This book is for anyone in a school improvement or leadership role.'
Janey Cooksley
Headteacher, Strategic English Lead and Teaching and Learning Lead.
David Ross Education Trust.

'No Silver Bullets resonates with me, the strategies are particularly useful for new Headteachers and those working in stand-alone schools.'
Becky Walker
Primary Director.
West Norfolk Academies Trust.

'*No Silver Bullets* offers a valuable and pragmatic approach to ensuring that school improvement strategies 'stick'.
Paul Ainsworth's new book presents a range of possible improvement actions that can be pursued with unfailing focus and attention, '*day in, day out*'.
The distinctive approach of *No Silver Bullets* is to emphasise the importance of *how* improvement actions, when tailored to a school's specific context and needs, are implemented. Each strategy in the book is matched with a carefully considered choice of systematic evaluation tools for leaders to adopt.
Grounded in Paul Ainsworth's extensive experience and expertise, this book will be an invaluable resource to any school leader seeking to make sustainable improvements in their school community.'
Zoë Elder, author of '*Full On Learning*'

'The title of the book is perfect – there are no 'silver bullets' but this strips the mammoth beast of school improvement back to a toolkit that focuses on doing fewer things really well. No bandwagons to jump on, just relentless consistency in tried and tested strategies to provide a great education for all learners.'
Donna Tandy
Deputy Chief Executive Officer
Focus Trust.

'Paul's supportive manner and insightful, practical advice has been of great value to teachers across all phases of the education sector. During my time working with him as CEO of a large MAT, his guidance was always in great demand amongst my headteachers, and I have no doubt that this book, which provides simple and easy-to-access advice to school leaders, will be very much welcomed by many.'
Rowena Hackwood
CEO Astrea Academy Trust.

'School improvement is hard as the title in No Silver Bullets suggest. It happens through people in Schools with the actions they take day in, day out; often subtle, unseen and not glamorous but it makes a difference to children's lives. This book provides a practical, insightful and knowledgeable overview of School Improvement. There are no Silver Bullets but there are certain aspects and elements that do work that should be considered outlined by Paul's extensive experience from working in and with Schools across the UK. There is something in this book for everyone, from the Senior Leader to Newly Qualified Teacher. A book to not just read once but act as a reference, challenge and reflection as to where you are at on your School Improvement journey and context. Highly recommended and it has already had me thinking of areas we can improve.'
Stephen Logan,
Deputy Head, Malet Lambert School.

'Paul has years of experience of - and is passionate about - school improvement. He has worked with numerous school leaders to ensure sustained improvement. This book is a must have for any school leader looking to bring about positive change, with tried & tested ideas.'
Liz White,
School Improvement Advisor.

'Provocatively titled 'No Silver Bullets: Day, in day out school improvement', this book creates the right cognitive conditions for thinking about school improvement. Refreshingly, Paul argues that there is no box of tricks or 'silver bullets.' School improvement is about effort, every day, keeping the main thing the main thing! Each page bristles with rich examples of school improvement in action that leaders can dip in and out of. A must read for any leader!'
Abby Bayford
Director of the ATT Institute.

'Everything I know of Paul's work is nothing but excellence and 'No Silver Bullets is no different'
Julie Keyes
The Education Consultant.

'No Silver Bullets is a reassuring and realistic message that school improvement relies on day to day hard work and clear focus and not an external quick fix being adopted by the school.'
Leann Lynch,
Strategic Teaching and Learning Leader,
L.E.A.D. Equate Teaching School Alliance.

'With so many people searching for the "quick fix" when it comes to developing and improving schools. Paul Ainsworth has hit the nail on the head with "No Silver Bullets"- Day in, day out School Improvement. It's not about the single new development or attention-grabbing strategy it's about deploying small, consistent approaches that aggregate over time to something much bigger. It's about the daily actions that collectively turn around the fortunes of schools and the children they serve.
"No Silver Bullets" is an excellent guide to key strategies that really make a difference when it comes to school improvement from someone who "walks the talk" with school leaders each and every day. A must-read for new and existing leaders ambitious to improve their schools.'
Gavin Booth,
CEO
Infinity Academies Trust

'The central message of 'no silver bullets' is essential for genuine school improvement. It requires persistence, day-in, day-out, returning to key ideas and embedding approaches."
John Bocking,
School Improvement for CEO's and Trust leaders.

Printed in Great Britain
by Amazon

85208934R00131